CREATION

"Books on faith and science typically fall into one of two categories: they either mock religion, dismissing it as myth and superstition, or they mock science, doubting conclusions widely affirmed by experts. It's rare to find a book that rises above this crossfire and instead values both faith *and* science, shedding light on *both* disciplines in mutually enhancing ways. I don't know anyone today writing on God, religion, and science with a more winsome, accessible, refreshing, and theologically rich perspective than Christopher Baglow. In this illuminating book, he touches on several hot-button issues that interface between science and faith—evolution, the problem of evil and suffering, divine and human freedom, and love—showing how the narratives offered by science and Christian theology are not contradictory, nor merely compatible, but are in fact harmonious stories told by the same author: God. If you know a young person who thinks science disproves faith, this is the book they need—get it to them."

Brandon Vogt
Senior content director at Word on Fire Catholic Ministries

"*Creation* not only demolishes the tired old canard that the Catholic faith is antithetical to science but also proposes a rigorous harmonization of the two, in which one need not regard with suspicion modern scientific understanding of evolution nor replace the authentic Catholic faith with an oversimplified cartoon caricature. Theologian Christopher Baglow confronts the details of modern scientific findings on the physical and biological evolution of the cosmos with the salvation history of humankind as laid out in the scriptures. The result is a reasoned, authentic, and uplifting description of the destiny awaiting each human being as a product of the cosmos and of God's infinite love for his creation."

Jonathan Lunine
Vice president of the Society of Catholic Scientists

"With clarity, ease, and beauty, Christopher Baglow composes a gift for modern Catholics: the dazzling wonder of the fullness of truth. As a teacher and writer, I have fresh reverence for the rational harmony of faith and science. As a human person, I find deep satisfaction in this joyful exploration of the Creator's universe and of humanity's true origins and destiny. This is a journey of faith seeking reason that is at once abundant and accessible."

Aimee Boudreaux MacIver
Catholic author and high school teacher

Books in the Engaging Catholicism series from the McGrath Institute for Church Life at the University Notre Dame help readers discover the beauty and truth of the Catholic faith through a concise exploration of the Church's most important but often difficult-to-grasp doctrines as well as crucial pastoral and spiritual practices. Perfect for seekers and new Catholics, clergy and catechetical leaders, and everyone in between, the series expands the McGrath Institute's mission to connect the Catholic intellectual life at Notre Dame to the pastoral life of the Church and the spiritual needs of her people.

Praise for the Engaging Catholicism series:

"The Engaging Catholicism series offers clear and engaging presentations of what we Catholics believe and how we practice our faith. These books are written by experts who know how to keep things accessible yet substantive, and there is nothing fluffy or light about them. They should be in the hand of anyone who simply wants to live their faith more deeply every day and to share it with others who teach, pastor, or parent."

Katie Prejean McGrady
Catholic author, speaker, and host of the *Ave Explores* podcast

"The Engaging Catholicism series is a powerful tool to bring the beauty and depth of our Catholic theological tradition to those who need it most. This series will help many to truly engage our Catholic faith."

Most Rev. Andrew Cozzens
Auxiliary Bishop of Saint Paul and Minneapolis

ENGAGING CATHOLICISM

CREATION

A Catholic's Guide to God and the Universe

Christopher T. Baglow

McGrath Institute for Church Life | University of Notre Dame

AVE MARIA PRESS AVE Notre Dame, Indiana

Nihil Obstat: Reverend Monsignor Michael Heintz, PhD, *Censor librorum*

Imprimatur: Most Reverend Kevin C. Rhoades, Bishop of Fort Wayne-South Bend

Given at Fort Wayne, Indiana, April 20, 2021

Founded in 1865, Ave Maria Press is a ministry of the United States Province of Holy Cross.

www.avemariapress.com

Paperback: ISBN-13 978-1-64680-107-7

E-book: ISBN-13 978-1-64680-108-4

Cover image © Rene Mattes / mauritius images GMBH / Alamy Stock Photo.

Cover and text design by Samantha Watson.

Printed and bound in the United States of America.

Library of Congress Cataloging-in-Publication Data
Names: Baglow, Christopher T., 1968- author.
Title: Creation : a Catholic's guide to God and the universe / Christopher
  T. Baglow.
Description: Notre Dame, Indiana : Ave Maria Press, [2021] | Series:
  Engaging Catholicism | Includes bibliographical references. | Summary:
  "This book explores the Christian doctrine of creation as both a
  profound asset to science and the ultimate cause of humility before God.
  Christian doctrine addresses the why of creation, making it perfectly
  hospitable to science, which can only help answer the how"-- Provided by
  publisher.
Identifiers: LCCN 2021024421 (print) | LCCN 2021024422 (ebook) | ISBN
  9781646801077 (paperback) | ISBN 9781646801084 (ebook)
Subjects: LCSH: Creation. | Catholic Church--Doctrines. | Creationism. |
  Religion and science. | BISAC: RELIGION / Christianity / Catholic |
  RELIGION / Religion & Science
Classification: LCC BT695 .B34 2021 (print) | LCC BT695 (ebook) | DDC
  231.7/65--dc23
LC record available at https://lccn.loc.gov/2021024421
LC ebook record available at https://lccn.loc.gov/2021024422

CONTENTS

SERIES FOREWORD

Doctrine is probably not the first thing that comes to mind when we consider the pastoral work of the Church. We tend to presume that doctrine is abstract, of interest primarily to theologians and clergy whose vocation it is to contemplate lofty questions of belief. On the other hand, we tend to think the pastoral life of the Church is consumed primarily with practical questions: How do we pray? How do we pass on faith to the next generation? How do we form Christians to care about the hungry and thirsty? How might our parishes become spaces of lived discipleship? What are the best practices for the formation of Catholic families? Presenting at catechetical conferences in dioceses on a specific point of Catholic theology, faculty and staff of the McGrath Institute for Church Life often hear the question, "So, what's the significance? Give me the practical takeaways."

The separation between doctrine and practice is bad for theologians, pastoral leaders, and Christians looking to grow in holiness. It leads to theologians who no longer see their vocation as connected to the Church. Academic theologians speak a language that the enlightened alone possess. On occasion, they turn their attention to the ordinary beliefs and practices of the faithful, sometimes reacting with amusement or horror that one could

be so primitive as to adore the Eucharist or leave flowers before
Our Lady of Guadalupe. The proper arena for the theologian to
exercise her craft is assumed to be the doctoral seminar, not the
parish or the Catholic secondary school.

Likewise, pastoral strategy too often develops apart from the
intellectual treasury of the Church. Such strategy is unreflective,
not able to critically examine its own assumptions. For example,
how we prepare adolescents for Confirmation is a theological and
pastoral problem. Without the wisdom of sacramental doctrine,
responding to this pastoral need becomes a matter of pragmatic
conjecture, unfortunately leading to the variety of both implicit
and often impoverished theologies of Confirmation that arose in
the twentieth century. Pastoral strategy divorced from the doc-
trinal richness of the Church can leave catechesis deprived of
anything worthwhile to pass on. If one is to be a youth minister,
it is not enough to know best practices for accompanying teens
through adolescence, since one can accompany someone even off
a cliff. Pastoral leaders must also know a good deal about what
Catholicism teaches to lead members of Christ's Body to the
fullness of human happiness.

The Engaging Catholicism series invites you to see the intrinsic and intimate connection between doctrine and the pastoral
life of the Church. Doctrines, after all, are the normative way of
handing on the mysteries of our faith. Doctrines make us able
to pick up a mystery, carry it around, and hand it to someone
else. Doctrines, studied and understood, allow us to know we *are*
handing on *this* mystery and not some substitute.

In order to properly hand on the mysteries of our faith, the
pastoral leader has to *know a given doctrine contains a mystery*—
has to have the doctrine opened up so that receiving it means

encountering the mystery it carries. Only then can one be transformed by the doctrine. The problem with religious practice unformed or inadequately formed by doctrine is that it expects an easy and mostly continuous spiritual high, which cannot be sustained if one has sufficient grasp of one's own humanity. We in the McGrath Institute for Church Life have confidence in Christian doctrines as saving truths, bearing mystery from the God who is love. We believe in the importance of these teachings for making us ever more human, and we believe in the urgent need to speak the Church's doctrines into, for, and with those who tend the pastoral life of the Church. We cannot think of any task more important than this. The books of this series represent our best efforts toward this crucial effort.

John C. Cavadini
Director of the McGrath Institute for Church Life
University of Notre Dame

INTRODUCTION

All of us are familiar with the all-too-common cultural meme that science and faith are enemies. This is called the *warfare* or *conflict model* of science and faith. According to this model, faith and science are rival, mutually exclusive ways of explaining the universe. The warfare model has become a deeply rooted assumption in the minds of many American Catholics and has taken a particularly strong hold on young people in recent decades. A 2014 study from the Center for the Study of Religion and Society and the National Study of Youth and Religion (NSYR) by sociologist Christian Smith discovered the following:

- Among Roman Catholic emerging adults in the study, 72 percent adopted the "inherent warfare" model of science and religion; that is, they considered them to be contradictory and incompatible.
- Among Roman Catholic emerging adults in the study, 62 percent said that their own views about religion have *not* been strengthened by the discoveries of science.
- Among Roman Catholic emerging adults in the study who have stopped practicing their faith, 78 percent cited the "conflict" of science and religion as one of the reasons why they no longer practice their faith.[1]

These findings were reinforced by a study released in 2016 by the Center for Applied Research in the Apostolate (CARA) at Georgetown University. The study focused on roughly the same age group as the NSYR and found the warfare model to be the typical attitude even among junior-high Catholic youth. Typical responses to questions included, "It [the Catholic faith] no longer fits what I understand of the universe" and "As I learn more about the world around me and understand things that I once did not, I find the thought of an all-powerful being to be less and less believable."[2] It is easy to see that these conclusions are not limited to the young, particularly when confronted with the understandings and convictions voiced by our children, students, and members of our youth groups.

Of course, this problem has produced a lot of hand-wringing and discouragement among many Catholic grandparents, parents, pastors, teachers, and catechists. It has also brought a swell of well-meaning but misinformed attempts to defend the Catholic faith in the face of scientific "secularism." Some, such as the Kolbe Center for the Study of Creation, have taken the route of rejecting modern science, joining forces (if not hands) with non-Catholic Evangelical outreaches such as the Creation Museum in Northern Kentucky. The Kolbe Center approach is referred to as creationism because of its insistence that God created the universe exactly (or almost exactly) according to their interpretation of the first and second creation accounts found in the book of Genesis (Gn 1–3). The Kolbe Center flatly rejects the modern scientific consensus and does so based on the (misunderstood) authority of the Bible, attacking "secular science" as atheistic and lacking solid evidence for its claims.

Creationism is a theological position; it claims to be the proper interpretation of the Bible and of the Christian doctrine of creation. Yet it has been rejected by the three most recent popes. In

1981 St. John Paul II noted that the Bible does not wish to give us a "scientific treatise," declaring that the Bible wishes to teach us theological truths, not scientific ones: "Any other teaching about the origin and make-up of the universe is alien to the intentions of the Bible, which does not wish to teach how heaven was made but how one goes to heaven."[3] In his Easter Vigil homily in 2011, Benedict XVI declared that the creation account in Genesis 1 "is not information about the external processes by which the cosmos and man himself came into being."[4] And in 2014, Pope Francis offered a similar rebuttal: "When we read the account of Creation in Genesis we risk imagining that God was a magician, complete with an all-powerful magic wand. But that was not so."[5] These quotes indicate that Catholics who embrace creationism do not represent the Church's understanding of creation. Arguing against well-established science simply by virtue of one's own interpretation of the Bible breaks faith and reason apart and fails to distinguish between science and theology.

So, rather than going on the offensive and rejecting science, how should Catholics respond to the warfare model? The first step is to recognize that young Catholics today are rarely, if ever, given a full explanation of what we mean when we call God "Creator," very often because their teachers, parents, and even grandparents themselves have never been adequately informed. All the way back in 1986, the future pope and renowned theologian Joseph Ratzinger lamented what he called "the suppression of faith in creation," noting that the theme of creation had been pushed to the margins of theology.[6] Because of this, Catholic catechesis on creation has become impoverished and defensive, for it lacks the confidence that understanding creates.

Young people need to be nourished by more than the assertion that God created the universe, and they certainly do not need that assertion bolstered by anti-science polemics and pseudo-scientific arguments. Instead, they need to understand that the God of Love whom they encounter in Jesus Christ is the same God who causes the universe to exist and that he can be encountered through it precisely because we know so much more about it today than ever before, thanks to science.

For all those who, like me, absolutely love both my Catholic faith and the grand adventure that is science, may this book be an opportunity to learn something new about God and the universe. And for all those given the precious duty of educating young people in the faith, may this book be an opportunity to enrich your understanding of the Christian doctrine of creation for your own sake as well as for the sake of those you serve. Throughout this text, the great discoveries of modern science will be taken as a catalyst, not an obstacle, to celebrate our faith in God the Creator in new, often surprising ways. We will begin with the doctrine of creation itself, then proceed to theological questions and insights both old and new. All will be undertaken in the spirit of St. John Paul II's vision of a "relational unity" between faith and science. As we ready ourselves to begin, let us call to mind and heart the memorable words he penned in 1988 to Fr. George Coyne, S.J., director of the Vatican Observatory: "Science can purify religion from error and superstition; religion can purify science from idolatry and false absolutes. Each can draw the other into a wider world, a world in which both can flourish."[7]

This book is dedicated to the memory of Richard Baglow, my loving and devoted father who first introduced me to the beauty of creation, bringing me fishing, camping, canoeing, and (my favorite!) bodysurfing. May this book help all who read it catch the wave of divine creation rippling through and manifested in all things.

1.

LOVE IS THE REASON: UNDERSTANDING THE CHRISTIAN DOCTRINE OF CREATION

> Do you want to know what goes on in the core of the
> Trinity? I will tell you. In the core of the Trinity the
> Father laughs and gives birth to the Son. The Son laughs
> back at the Father and gives birth to the Spirit. The
> whole Trinity laughs and gives birth to us.
>
> —Meister Eckhart[1]

This quote from the Dominican preacher Meister Eckhart (ca. 1260–ca. 1328) is one of my favorite images of divine creation. To understand the laughter he refers to, set aside any idea of laughter that comes at the expense of another, or at the expense of truth or goodness, and think about a moment of pure hilarity shared among friends, one in which togetherness is unclouded by vanity or insult and in which laughter is the fruit of joy, born of bonds of love. This is why the universe exists—for that kind of laughter, or rather, the uncaused, eternal perfection of divine happiness, which that selfless laughter reflects.

When I was a teenager back in the early 1980s, laughter of a much different kind was why a much different "account" of creation was my absolute favorite. It begins with familiar biblical-sounding words: "In the beginning, the universe was created," but then throws a hilarious punchline: "This has made a lot of people very angry and has been widely regarded as a bad move." Thus begins the second book in Douglas Adams's *The Hitchhiker's Guide to the Galaxy* trilogy, a sci-fi comic classic, one of the funniest books I have ever read. The title of the series refers to a handbook for people who, using advanced technology, want to make their way around the Milky Way via space travel and time travel, visiting strange, exotic worlds and life-forms without getting themselves killed or mutilated or stranded in the wrong time period where they might accidentally become their own mother or father. In the five books of the trilogy (yes, you read that correctly!), Adams describes a universe whose basic thread is irrationality and meaninglessness, completely and only ruled by chance, and chronicles the adventures of people who roam that universe looking mostly for cheap thrills and, occasionally, a towel (thus the first rule of the *Hitchhiker's Guide*: when hitchhiking across the galaxy, never forget your towel).

When I read this satirical "creation account" for the first time, the Police had yet to break up, one could still make out Bob Dylan's lyrics at his concerts, and I was slowly wandering away from the Catholic faith of my upbringing. In the sentences immediately following the opening lines of the second book, I found what I thought was a slam-dunk indictment of what I had been taught about the doctrine that God is the Creator of all things:

> Many races believe that the universe was created by
> some sort of god, though the Jatravartid people of

> Viltvodle VI believe that the entire universe was in fact
> sneezed out of a being called the Great Green Arklesei-
> zure. The Jatravartids, who live in perpetual fear of the
> time they call The Coming of the Great White Hand-
> kerchief, are small blue creatures with more than 50
> arms each, who are therefore unique in being the only
> race in history to have invented the aerosol deodorant
> before the wheel.[2]

To my mind, what I thought Christians believe about creation
seemed just as fantastic and irrational as the Jatravartid creation
account. Christian belief also seemed fantastic and irrational
to Adams, who called himself a "radical atheist" and at whose
funeral Richard Dawkins, the famous biologist and New Atheism
anti-apostle, gave a eulogy.

Of course, I had an extremely superficial understanding of
the biblical accounts of creation, which are symbolic narratives
the depths and historical contexts of which I had not the slightest
clue. But although I had read the biblical creation accounts several times in Catholic school, no one had ventured to offer me the
best guide to these accounts—namely, the Church's proclamation
of the doctrine of creation in her teaching in what is called sacred
Tradition. Sacred Tradition is the very "life and consciousness" of
the Church. This "life and consciousness" is caused by the Holy
Spirit, who dwells in her and unites her to Christ as his body. The
Holy Spirit is the one whom Christ himself promised to send:
"The Advocate, the holy Spirit that the Father will send in my
name—he will teach you everything and remind you of all that
[I] told you" (Jn 14:26). While sacred scripture is the Word of
God given long ago, sacred Tradition is nothing less than Jesus
Christ, the Word of God, living within his Church throughout

history and in the *here and now*. Therefore, Scripture does not stand alone—we discover the meaning of Scripture through the Church's teaching.

In this chapter we will consider what sacred Tradition, as embodied in the Church's professions of faith throughout the centuries, teaches us to understand about the divinely revealed truth that God is the Creator of all things, "visible and invisible." As we do, I will refer back to the Jatravartid "creation account," Douglas Adams's funny but misconceived jab at Christian belief, to show how it is the polar opposite of the Christian doctrine of creation. In fact, this entire chapter should be understood as a point-by-point polemic against the Jatravartid creation narrative. I feel this approach is quite appropriate, considering that the very first creation account in the Bible was *also* written as a polemic against a different, much more serious, but equally pagan creation account, as we will discover at the end of this chapter. But let me begin by summarizing the Christian doctrine of creation:

- The Jatravartids saw creation as something coming into being from some greater being, the Great Green Arkleseizure (suffering from a divine bout of flu). But Christians see creation as *ex nihilo*, literally "from NO-thing," and above all do not see God as a being, not even the Supreme Being, but as the Source of Being to all things.

- The Jatravartids saw creation as a process, something with a beginning, middle, and end (like a sneeze: Aaaah-CHOO!). But Christians see creation as an eternal act, one that brings time itself into existence along with all beings and affects every moment of time; creation is not *in time* but *with time* (*cum tempore*).

- The Jatravartids saw creation as an accident, unintentional, reflexive, a sneeze. Christians see no necessity on the part of God to create—creation is *ex libertate*, out of the perfect freedom of God. And Creation is intentional; it is willed by God.
- Finally, and most tragically, the Jatravartids saw creation as a solitary process—a sneeze is something covered up, something that causes us to apologize, as in: "Pardon me for soiling your shirt!" But Christians believe creation to be from the Trinity, *ex Trinitate*, and so it is the overflow of perfect, self-giving love and togetherness. I will show that creation is something like an act of mercy that causes us and all things to be, although to understand why will take a bit of explaining.

The Christian doctrine of creation, then, involves four component truths: God creates the universe (1) from nothing, (2) with time (vs. "in time"), (3) freely, and (4) as Trinity. None of these is the product of human discovery, but each is the product of divine revelation. These truths were solemnly professed and defined by the Catholic Church at three ecumenical councils: Lateran IV in 1215, Florence in 1442, and Vatican I in 1869–1870. Ecumenical councils are assemblies at which bishops from the whole world come together to authoritatively teach in union with the pope regarding matters of faith and morals. Catholics recognize that when bishops are gathered in councils by the pope, they have "the charism of infallibility" from the Holy Spirit. Thanks to this special and unique grace, they together exercise freedom from error in definitive acts of teaching on matters of faith and morals, and their teaching requires the unswerving "assent of faith," since God has definitively spoken through them.[3] Therefore, the four elements listed above are integral to the Christian faith. Let us start with the most baffling of the four: creation "from nothing."

CREATION, NOT CHANGE

The Jatravartid cosmology is one in which lesser beings come from some greater being. But foundational to the Christian doctrine of creation is that God is beyond the ordinary meaning of the term "being"; therefore, we misunderstand God when we try to understand God as a being. For Christians, God is *not* the Supreme Being. Rather, God is the Source of Being, the Giver of Reality to all things. Beings can be comprehended and, as Augustine once said, if you comprehend it, it is certainly not God.[4]

My favorite example of the humility involved in this Christian understanding of God is in a fictional dialogue written in 1444 by the philosopher, theologian, bishop, and cardinal Nicholas of Cusa (1401–1464). He called this work "On the Hidden God" (*De Deo Abscondito*). In it a pagan approaches a Christian whom he finds at prayer. When the pagan asks the Christian to identify the God he worships, he receives a startling answer:

> The *Pagan* spoke: I see that you have most devoutly prostrated yourself and are shedding tears of love—not hypocritical tears but heartfelt ones. Who are you, I ask?
> *Christian*: I am a Christian.
> *Pagan*: What are you worshipping?
> *Christian*: God.
> *Pagan*: Who is [this] God whom you worship?
> *Christian*: I don't know.
> *Pagan*: How is it that you worship so seriously that of which you have no knowledge?
> *Christian*: Because I am without knowledge [of Him], I worship Him.[5]

The paradox is stunning—only a God who *cannot* be fully comprehended, who is inexpressible Truth, could be the true God and worthy of our adoration. And so it is with the doctrine of creation—it is not susceptible to comprehension. I note this here because the first element of the doctrine—that is, creation from nothing—is misunderstood precisely when we try to comprehend it, to fit it into our tiny minds.

In the many presentations I give on faith and science, I make a distinction between "how" and "why" questions and answers. I am very fond of a quote from Rabbi Jonathan Sacks, who once wrote, "Science takes things apart to tell us how they work; religion brings things together to show us what they mean."[6] But St. John Paul II said it first; in his words, "The theological teaching of the Bible, like the doctrine of the Church . . . does not seek so much to teach us the *how* of things, as rather the *why* of things."[7] The deepest reason for making this distinction is to explain the Christian doctrine of creation *ex nihilo*—"from nothing." God uses no preexisting material to create the universe, so no "how" explanations are possible to describe the act of creation. His act of creation causes everything to exist, including matter, space, time, and even the very laws that govern the universe. Without God's constant divine action, there would literally be "no thing," as well as no space and no time, whatsoever. God, in one eternal act, creates and sustains all that exists, from the cosmic explosion of the Big Bang and the celestial formation of the billions of galaxies that are flying through space, to the evolution of planetary life and the formation of the earth's majestic mountain ranges, to the fly that is buzzing around me as I type this. Time and space are not determinative factors when it comes to God's divine activity of creation, because "a thousand years in [God's] eyes are merely a day gone by" (Ps 90:4).

The mystery of creation *ex nihilo* is captured nowhere more beautifully than in a quote from G. K. Chesterton, who compares God's act of creation of each and every thing out of nothing to the exuberance and love of repetition we see in young children. When a child wants a parent to push them on the swing for hours, saying, "Do it again! Do it again! Do it again!" their exuberance shows an overflow of life (while the parent's weariness shows that stress and anxieties and age have taken a lot of that exuberance away!). But like a young child, God does not tire of creating each and every thing at each and every moment:

> It is possible that God says every morning, "Do it again" to the sun; and every evening, "Do it again" to the moon. It may not be automatic necessity that makes all daisies alike; it may be that God makes every daisy separately, but has never got tired of making them. It may be that He has the eternal appetite of infancy; for we have sinned and grown old, and our Father is younger than we.[8]

Chesterton's poetic imagery is true—with unlimited divine youthfulness and energy, God creates every daisy and causes every sunrise. He does so without ceasing because he is holding all things in existence through his perfect, eternal act of creation *ex nihilo*. In the words of the Letter to the Hebrews, "By faith we understand that the universe was ordered by the word of God, so that what is visible came into being through the invisible" (Heb 11:3).

We might be tempted to ask, "*How* does God cause creatures to exist and the universe to be real?" But this is dead-end thinking. "How" answers involve processes that occur in time and can be studied by science. But God is eternal and unchanging; time is something he creates. God's reality is a perfect *now* with no past or future. In his perfect eternity God wills his creatures to be, and because he does so, they are. No process is involved in divine creation; as St. Thomas Aquinas says, God is "the cause hidden from every human being."[9] There is, however, a crucial distinction between primary and secondary causality. God causes all things to be, and so God should be called the *Primary Cause*. But in causing all things to be, God causes them in such a way that they are able to be causes of each other in various ways. For example, parents are the real biological causes of their children, giving them a particular *kind* of existence as this or that kind of animal. But it is God who gives *being* to both the parents and their offspring.

Once we recognize this distinction, it becomes clear that the doctrine of creation *ex nihilo* is perfectly hospitable to science precisely because it is not a "how" explanation—that is, not a scientific one. God's creative act is not a change, so it cannot be studied in the way changes are studied. This preserves scientific and theological explanations from bleeding into, substituting for, or competing with each other. Scientists rightly become upset when believers try to stick God into the processes of the universe as a "how" explanation, as creationists do. The evolutionary biologist Richard Lewontin once said in a *New York Times* article that all scientists must embrace materialism to avoid allowing the "Divine Foot in the door."[10] To Lewontin, if you allow for the existence of God, then you have nothing left for science to study, because who knows what tricks God might be playing with the universe or with your laboratory! And yet materialism is not necessary to protect the integrity of the natural world. Creation *ex nihilo* means that God is the cause of the existence, the reality, of all things, not that God is an all-powerful, magical substitute for natural causes. He answers the ultimate questions: "Why does anything exist at all?" and "Why is the universe orderly and yet open?"—not questions like "How did mammals evolve?" or "How did the universe develop during the Big Bang?" Science takes care of those "how" questions, and the more science can explain, the more it shows God's majesty as Creator.

On the other hand, some believers get upset when atheists, such as the late Christopher Hitchens, reject the existence of God because they assume that science has squeezed God out of the gaps in our knowledge of how the universe works. "Thanks to the telescope and the microscope, religion no longer offers an explanation of anything important," declared Hitchens, as if that settles everything.[11] That is a serious problem for the Great Green Arkleseizure, but not for the one true God, the God of Christianity. Christians do not believe in a God of the Gaps who explains this or that natural phenomenon, but in a God who, beyond our greatest genius and wildest dreams, is the ultimate reason for the existence of all things, constantly upholding them in being, allowing and enabling them to cause each other in a beautiful, sometimes perplexing, always amazing universe.

Let's conclude this section on creation *ex nihilo* with a quote from St. John Paul II:

> "Creation" therefore means: to make from nothing, to call into existence, that is, to form a being from nothing. . . . Through this creative power (omnipotence)

> God is in the creature and the creature is in him. How-
> ever, this divine immanence in no way diminishes God's
> transcendence in regard to everything to which he gives
> existence.[12]

This final quote captures something beautiful that also sharp-
ly distinguishes Christian from Jatravartid theology. Because
God forms us from nothing and holds us in existence at every
moment, he is within all things, large and small. As St. Augustine
wrote in his *Confessions*, God is more present to us than we are to
ourselves. A sneeze expels what it produces outward, away from
its source. But God is close, always, even though he also utterly
transcends his creation. As an unknown Jesuit once said in a
eulogy for St. Ignatius, "Not to be encompassed by the greatest,
but to allow oneself to be encompassed by the smallest—that is
divine."[13]

THE DIVINE NOW

The Jatravartid theologians look back gratefully to a moment
when, thanks to blind luck, the universe came into existence
through the Great Green Arkleseizure, in whose snot they live,
and move, and have their being. That moment was when the
Great Green Arkleseizure acted; after that, the deed was done. The
late, great physicist Stephen Hawking once assumed that Christians also think of divine creation as something that happened
"back then." In 2010 he declared that "theology has been made
irrelevant by physics," and in 2018 he explained what he meant:
"So when people ask me if a god created the universe, I tell them
the question itself makes no sense. Time didn't exist before the
Big Bang, so there was no time for God to make the universe

in."[14] In a sense, the temporal language of our biblical creation accounts, which we so often translate as "In the beginning," may have misled him here, for no human, not even one as brilliant as the late Stephen Hawking, can directly conceive of a reality that doesn't involve time. But what Hawking failed to see is that the Christian doctrine of creation is very different from any temporal account of *how* the universe began. It has to do not with the first moment in time, but with the very origin of time itself and with God's perfect eternity.

The Church's doctrine of creation includes the profession that the universe was created "with time." This phrase should be interpreted as identifying *every moment* as the result of the divine act of creation. Since God is eternal, his creative act is itself timeless. The term "with time" (*cum tempore*) has been used by the Church and her theologians to emphasize that time only exists in relation to creatures, not God. It is a feature of the universe and is itself a created reality that simultaneously accompanies the creation of physical matter.

Creation *with time* means that every moment is the moment of creation, from the first moment of the universe's existence until now. All things are being brought into existence out of nothing by God *right now*. Because God transcends time, God's act of creating at the first moment of the universe is no different than what God is doing at this moment. Right now, as much as at any time in the past, God is saying, "Let there be light," "Let the earth teem with living things," and so on. God's act of creation is not a historical event that happens within time, but it is instead a metaphysical reality describing the universe's dependence on God's eternal act of creating, which transcends time.

The particle physicist Stephen Barr offers an analogy to help us understand the timelessness of divine creation—the analogy of a playwright such as Shakespeare.[15] Shakespeare's *Romeo and Juliet* opens with these lines: "Two households, both alike in dignity, / In fair Verona, where we lay our scene, / From ancient grudge break to new mutiny, / Where civil blood makes civil hands unclean."[16] That is the *beginning* of *Romeo and Juliet*; it references a point in time when the play begins in Shakespeare's fictional Verona. But Shakespeare is the *origin* of those lines and everything else in *Romeo and Juliet*. When sacred scripture speaks of God acting "in the beginning" or before it, it is pointing to God as the *origin* of the universe and history, not to some moment in the past. Sacred scripture uses temporal language to communicate this truth, not because God's creative act is a temporal one, but because of the poverty of human language to describe it. We must think of words like "in the beginning" (Gn 1:1) or "before the foundation of the world" (Eph 1:4) not as literal designations but as metaphysical placeholders, which are there not to get us looking at a calendar or a clock but to bring us to contemplate the ultimate, timeless origin of all things.

It is true that divine revelation also points to a first moment for our universe. That's a truth that is important for us, but not for scientific reasons. It is important because it tells us that the universe we live in is subject to a narrative, although we do not know all of the details of that narrative. Just like salvation history, the universe has a purpose toward which it has been moving, in fits and starts, since whenever it began. And the story of our salvation is to that longer narrative the decisive turning point, the chapter which reveals what the whole story is about. Thankfully, we do not await the Coming of the Great White Handkerchief, but a "new heaven and a new earth" (Rv 21:1) in which all things will be conformed to the glory of Christ's resurrection and in which God will "be all in all" (1 Cor 15:28).

BORN OF FREEDOM

The Jatravartids await a free act by which their universe will be "wiped" out (pun intended!). But to their thinking the origin of the universe is an accident, something unintentional, not something willed or the result of freedom. Once again their creation story departs from the Christian profession of faith, which is that the universe is freely created by God. It is something willed, desired to be by God. Pope Benedict XVI was getting at this when in the inaugural homily of his papacy he declared, "We are not some casual and meaningless product of evolution. Each of us is the result of a thought of God. Each of us is willed. Each of us is loved. Each of us is necessary."[17] Before any scientists get nervous, let me add that, two years and a few months later, he also said, "There is a great deal of scientific proof in favor of evolution, which appears as a reality that we must see and that enriches our knowledge of life and of being as such."[18] In other words, he was not denying evolution. He was denying that we are *only* casual and meaningless products of it, that ultimately we are just a cosmic accident.

The pope was thinking, no doubt, of the First Creation Account, where we read that God said, "Let us make human beings in our image, after our likeness" (Gn 1:26). This very human image of God mulling over the prospect of making human beings points to divine freedom—that God freely created humans and the entire universe. In the words of Psalm 135:6–7,

"Whatever the LORD desires he does in heaven and on earth, in the seas and all depths." In the same vein, the First Vatican Council (1869–1870) proclaimed:

> [The] one true God, by his goodness and almighty power, [brought things into being] not with the intention of increasing his happiness, nor indeed of obtaining happiness, but in order to manifest his perfection by the good things which he bestows on what he creates, by *an absolutely free plan*.[19]

Let's reflect on what this implies. First of all, it means that God is free either to create the cosmos or not to create it. It also means that God is not obligated to create the best possible universe. God is not forced to create one possible universe out of all possible universes because it is "best." This shows God's radical difference from us. As creatures with a capacity to develop toward perfection, there is always a tendency to choose the best, and choosing the best is always preferable and sometimes morally necessary. But God cannot be perfected and is not perfected through creating—he is already perfect Goodness. Furthermore, God has pledged himself to bringing his creation to its fullest possible perfection. In the words of the *Catechism,* "With infinite power God could always create something better. But with infinite wisdom and goodness God freely willed to create a world 'in a state of journeying' towards its ultimate perfection."[20]

The perfect freedom by which God creates also means that the universe was created out of perfect love. God, who is Love (see 1 John 4:8), chose to make this universe, and he did so without being under any coercion or necessity, which means that God did not *have* to create in order to be God. The International

Theological Commission, the pope's theological "think-tank," emphasizes the personal nature of this free choice of God, who makes the whole universe for the sake of humanity: "[The doctrine of creation] teach[es] us that the existing universe is the setting for a radically personal drama, in which the triune Creator calls out of nothingness those to whom He then calls out in love."[21]

If the world is the product of freedom, does it not make sense that it is not a deterministic algorithm, with zillions and zillions of bits of code but no spontaneity? Should we not expect something like evolution, in which the universe freely develops, and which ultimately produces creatures capable of the exercise of freedom—namely, human beings? If so, that means that our loving God is never coercive; he never forces creation into a rigid program with no stain, no tinge, no possibility of tragedy or suffering. Just as God is free, he not only makes the universe freely, but makes it the arena of freedom. This makes love possible, but it also makes evil possible.

Most importantly, divine freedom finds its most powerful realization in self-giving, sacrificial love. This brings us to our final element, which is the most important, the one that, once understood, contains all the others.

LOVE IS THE REASON

For the Jatravartids, a solitary Supreme Being, obviously more complex and more powerful than themselves, gave rise to their universe and themselves. To understand how different the Christian doctrine of creation is, remember the words of Meister Eckhart with which we began this chapter: "The whole Trinity laughs and gives birth to us." Laughter is not a solitary reality; it is a communal one, one of shared life, perspective, and joy. It takes more than one person for this kind of joyous hilarity. And we know that there is more than one divine person in God—God is a unity but also a community.

In the profession of creation by the Trinity, we see that each divine person is mysteriously revealed in all that exists. The Son-*Logos* is the "Mind" or "Reason" to whom we attribute the orderliness of the universe. The Holy Spirit, the Gift-Love of God, is the one to whom we attribute its openness. To the Father—who eternally begets the Son, both of whom the Spirit eternally proceeds from—is attributed the very power by which the universe exists. Though we attribute these various actions to one of each of the three divine persons, creation is a unified action on the part of the whole divine Trinity. As the Council of Ferrara-Florence proclaimed in 1442, "The one true God, Father, Son and Holy Spirit, is the creator of all things that are."[22]

The Holy Trinity is a perfect communion of love, which means that the universe is the product of divine love and goodness. St. Thomas Aquinas offers a distinction that is very helpful in capturing the weight of this. He teaches that there are (at least) two kinds of love: the love that is justice and the love that is mercy. As we consider this quote, ask yourself which kind of love fits with the idea of creation we have developed thus far:

> When a person's love is caused by the goodness of the one he loves, then that person loves out of justice— it is just that he loves such a person. When, however, love causes goodness in the beloved, then it is a love springing from mercy. The love with which God loves

us produces goodness in us; hence mercy is . . . *the root of divine love.*[23]

Let's explore this. *Justice* is the giving to another what is due to them. When I love and respect a great person, such as a saint, I am not being merciful to them; I am being just—their goodness *causes* my love. Similarly, when I give my children my time and attention, I am not primarily being merciful to them; I am simply being just—I am giving them what is theirs by right. These things can be called love, but this is loving out of justice because love is what is due. In these cases, those who receive love have a right to it.

But what about when I forgive an offense committed against me and am friendly to a person who has hurt me? What about when I refuse to retaliate with insult or injury and, instead, offer a kind word? Or when I give freely to the poor, going beyond the limits of strict justice and expending myself so that they may have a better life? This is a love that actually isn't caused by goodness, which is the love that occurs out of justice. Instead, this love causes goodness where it is absent, "a love springing from mercy."

Which of these resonates more with the doctrine of creation? Nothing can be good unless it exists, and nothing is owed to something that doesn't exist. As we have already seen, God creates the universe *ex nihilo*, out of nothing. He causes good things to exist not out of any justice to them but out of something like mercy. Therefore, divine mercy, "the root of divine love," is the reason for the universe and everything in it. We are created out of divine mercy, in which God causes goodness where goodness is absent. The great English mystic Julian of Norwich portrays this beautifully in a vision she was given in prayer:

> The Holy Spirit showed me a little thing, the size of
> a hazelnut, lying in the palm of my hand, and to my
> understanding it was as round as any ball. I looked
> upon it and thought, "What may this be?" And I was
> answered, "It is everything that exists." I marveled how
> it could endure, for I thought it would certainly fall
> into nothingness because of its littleness. And I was
> answered, *"It lasts and always shall, because God loves
> it, and all things have being through the love of God."*[24]

It is here that we have arrived at the heart of the Christian
doctrine of creation. Nothing is unless it is created, and everything created exists because of God's inexhaustible, merciful love.
God had no need to create, no hunger to fill by creating. Rather,
the universe is the product of love overflowing, and merciful love
is therefore the foundation and deepest meaning of all things, the
same mercy with which the world is redeemed by Christ on the
Cross. Creation and redemption spring from the same source,
and the Cross of Christ is the very meaning of the whole universe,
the key to why it exists and how to find our own meaning and
purpose within it.

The Creator is Love and creates only for the sake of love. This
is what I wish someone had explained to me when I was young.
Although I still enjoy the humor of Douglas Adams, I now know
what the real punchline is. The Jatravartid theology of creation
is funny not because it is like the Christian doctrine of creation,
but because it is so unlike it; in fact, it is its polar opposite. The
Great Green Arkleseizure of Douglas Adams bears no resemblance
to the God of Jesus Christ.

THE FIRST CREATION ACCOUNT

It may seem strange to some readers that, in covering the Christian doctrine of creation, I have quoted more atheists than I have quoted sacred scripture. But that's only because, like Jesus, I wanted to save the best for last. The polemic I have offered you is my modern interpretation of the polemic that begins the Bible, the First Creation Account found in Genesis 1:1–2:4.

Much biblical scholarship has been dedicated to understanding the context in which the First Creation Account was written, and most scholars suggest that, due to its language and style, it took its final form around the middle of the sixth century BC. Although no one knows the name(s) of the inspired author(s), some creative thinking can help us establish a possible, but not certain, scenario for its composition.

Imagine that you are a Jew living more than five hundred years before Christ. You are a priest, which is a duty of religious leadership bestowed by God upon your family line, a duty that you take as the primary purpose of your life. Your responsibilities are vital: offering sacrifices, leading the congregation in prayer, and maintaining a close adherence to the Law given by Moses, whom God raised up long ago to lead his people out of slavery in Egypt and into a land "flowing with milk and honey" (Dt 26:9)—the Promised Land.

But you are no longer living in that land. It has been devastated by an invading empire. You, and all of God's people, have been forcibly removed from it and have been deported to live in the land of the very empire that took it from you—Babylon. The Temple, the place of God's presence, has been reduced to rubble. You now have a new duty—you must help your people hold on to their faith in God and to the way of life he gave to them, and you must do so against all odds.

It is in that place, during that terrible time that generations to come will call the Exile (597–539 BC), that you and your children hear these unsettling words:

> When in the height heaven was not named,
> And the earth beneath did not yet bear a name,
> Apsu, Fresh-Water, the Father of the Gods,
> And Tiamat, Salt-Water, Chaos, the mother of the Gods,
> Mingled their waters together . . .
> Then, in the midst of heaven, the gods were created . . .

These words begin the *Enûma Eliš* (ē-nooh-mah eh-lēsh), the Babylonian story of the world's creation and the central myth of the Babylonian religion.[25] It begins with a father god, Apsu, and a mother god, Tiamat, attempting to kill their own children. It continues with them instead being killed by their offspring and with the leader of those offspring, Marduk, making the earth and sky out of his mother's body parts. It ends with Marduk killing the dragon Kingu, Tiamat's lover and the commander of her army. As the blood of the dragon drips out, it is collected so that human beings can be formed out of it. Marduk then makes them to be slaves to all the gods, including the sun god, the moon god, and the star gods.

It is a story of violence and death, filled with deeds that are the polar opposite of the way the one true God, YHWH, acts. Slowly, but surely, a response is growing within you and within the other priests to this dreadfully warped picture of divinity and of the origin of human beings and the universe. Thanks to you, a different story will be heard by the people, a story with a very different beginning: "Bereshit bara Elohim et hashamayim ve'et ha'arets," "In the beginning the Lord-God [not Marduk] created the heavens and the earth" (Gen 1:1).

Much more can be said about the First Creation Account, and we will return to it in future chapters. For now, let's recognize it for what it is—a courageous polemic against an anti-human, oppressive pagan myth. Because it is so beautiful, it is easy to think of it as timeless, and in the deepest way, it is. But in its day it was also an act of cultural resistance, just as the Christian doctrine of creation must always be in a fallen world. Today it reads to us as a solemn, quiet sacred text, "like the tolling of a great old bell," as Joseph Ratzinger once put it.[26] But in its context it was as dramatic, even as revolutionary, as the Declaration of Independence must have been in 1776.

And it is chock-full of symbolism, which should indicate it is not a scientific treatise. For the sake of rejecting the erroneous creationist approach, which puts God's Word in conflict with the greatest scientific discoveries of modern times, let's simply identify the literary genre of the First Creation Account as a *symbolic cosmogony,* an account of the beginning and development of the universe that uses symbolism to show its deepest truth: the meaning of the universe and of our place within it. Unlike the Big Bang Theory, which is a *scientific cosmogony* that involves careful calculation to give us exact details about time, space, matter, and energy, or the *Enûma Eliš,* a *mythological cosmogony* in which symbolism is secondary and powerful gods and goddesses kill each other and make the universe and human slaves in the process, the First Creation Account is *primarily* symbolic, a great work of poetic imagination that captures a truth deeper than other modes of human writing can convey.

But the pagan authors of the *Enûma Eliš* were on to something—if their narrative of violence is not accurate to describe the divine Source of all things, it is a scarily accurate depiction of human life and what we see in the biosphere, then and now. If we are honest, it is hard to blame them for thinking that creaturely violence was begotten by divine violence. How can a universe filled with violence and pain be the product of perfect love? Addressing this will be our next task.

2.

THE POPE AND THE QUESTION: DIVINE CREATION AND THE PROBLEM OF EVIL

> Oh, that I knew where I might find him, that I might
> come even to his seat! I would learn what he would
> answer me, and understand what he would say to me.
> Would he contend with me in the greatness of his
> power? . . . Therefore I am terrified at his presence;
> when I consider, I am in dread of him. God has made
> my heart faint; the Almighty has terrified me.
>
> —Job 23:3, 5–6, 15–16

A POPE WHO QUESTIONS

In the last chapter I quoted the inaugural homily of Pope Benedict XVI. Of all that I have read by him (and I read everything that I can get my hands on by this great theologian), it is my favorite. It is not often recognized that in that homily, a pope finally asked and answered a question in front of an international viewing audience that I imagine millions of Catholics would love to have answered; indeed, I know of no Catholics who wouldn't want an answer, because every Catholic whom I know has asked the question themselves. It is Job's question in scripture, and so often it is our question too, whenever we see suffering or experience it ourselves.

Benedict set the stage for his question by referring to the pallium, woven in pure lamb's wool, which had just been set upon his shoulders, as others had been set upon the shoulders of every pope since the fourth century. He explained that the pallium refers to the participation of the bishop of Rome in the ministry of Jesus the Good Shepherd—the wool represents "the lost, sick or weak sheep which the shepherd places on his shoulders and carries to the waters of life." In other words, the wool pallium represents all of humanity, lost in the desert of sin and meaninglessness. Then Benedict offered a heroic image of Jesus, the Good Shepherd: "The Son of God will not let this happen; he cannot abandon humanity in such a wretched condition. He leaps to his feet and abandons the glory of heaven, in order to go in search of the sheep and pursue it, all the way to the Cross. He takes it upon his shoulders and carries our humanity; he carries us all—he is the good shepherd who lays down his life for the sheep."

Then Benedict made a contrast with the original ancient meaning of the king as a shepherd, showing how God's self-revelation in Christ gives it the surprising new meaning he is describing. Ancient Near Eastern kings cynically referred to themselves as shepherds because they could slaughter their flock as they wished. But Jesus is the true shepherd of all humanity, who lays down his life for them. As Benedict explained: "It is not power, but love that redeems us! This is God's sign: he himself is love."

And it was just here that he raised the question that encapsulated a hope that all of us have had at one time or another: "How often we wish that God would show himself stronger, that he would strike decisively, defeating evil and creating a better world." *Here it comes,* I thought. *Now the greatest Catholic theologian of our day, our newly minted pope for that matter, will speak to my deepest question, the one that so often haunts me in many forms.* "His people cry out, so why does God not act? Why does he remain silent? Why do the poor cry out and yet seemingly are given no reply, are not rescued from their oppressors, their murderers, their abusers? For that matter, why must they cry out when their innocence and happiness is shattered by the grotesque trauma of evil? Why does God not prevent it?"

At that moment, I had in mind many things: a beloved friend who had hung himself, the horrors of Auschwitz, the victims of serial killers, the victims of the terrible tsunami that just months before had killed 230,000 people. Just four months after the homily, a massive storm, Hurricane Katrina, would rage across the Gulf of Mexico and flood my home and almost destroy my beloved native city, New Orleans, sending my wife, my five-year-old daughter, my three-year-old son, and me into refugee status for a year—had I known it was coming, that would have been in my mind too.

And so I waited, and I listened, and I heard his answer, an answer that stunned me because it showed that my hope for a definitive answer, regardless of how reasonable it seemed to me, was not true hope, but my own impatience. Benedict continued:

> All ideologies of power justify themselves in exactly this way, they justify the destruction of whatever would stand in the way of progress and the liberation of humanity. We suffer on account of God's patience. And yet, we need his patience. God, who became a lamb, tells us that the world is saved by the Crucified One, not

by those who crucified him. *The world is redeemed by the patience of God. It is destroyed by the impatience of man.*[1]

"Ideologies of power." "The impatience of man." The pope's answer to my question was to question me, my way of thinking, so as to conform it to the standard of faith, the standard of the Crucified One. If I had ears to hear, I would've noticed that he had answered the question already even before he asked it when he said, "It is not power, but love that redeems us!" This was a moment of grace for me, because I realized that this refutation of my false hope was not a refutation of all hope. It was an invitation to a different, purer, more beautiful hope: the theological virtue of hope, which is a hope that does not simply call on the power of God to act from without, pushing salvation buttons the way creationists often conceive of him doing. Instead, it is a hope that calls on the love of God within, transforming me into one who, like Christ, finds salvation within suffering, who learns compassion and the courage not only to suffer but to suffer valiantly with others.

I was surprised by an entirely unexpected answer and the grace it offered, grace that has carried me through many tragedies since. But as the pope would say just a little bit further along in his homily, "There is nothing more beautiful than to be surprised by the Gospel, by the encounter with Christ. There is nothing more beautiful than to know Him and to speak to others of our friendship with Him. The task of the shepherd, the task of the fisher of men, can often seem wearisome. But it is beautiful and wonderful, because it is truly a service to joy, to God's joy which longs to break into the world." And how does God's joy break into the world? Not through power, but through love.

This would not be the last time Pope Benedict XVI would ask such a question—the next time he asked it, he asked it to God directly. Just a year after his inauguration he traveled to Auschwitz. Walking through the gate of terror alone, the gate that still bears the Nazi lie to their Jewish victims: *ARBEIT MACHT FREI* (WORK WILL MAKE YOU FREE), Benedict turned to the Lord, saying, "In a place like this, words fail; in the end, there can only be a dread silence—a silence which is itself a heartfelt cry to God: Why, Lord, did you remain silent? How could you tolerate all this?"[2]

So the problem of evil remains a question that only God can answer. When we consider what science has revealed about the universe, everything we now know has only sharpened the problem of evil, even as that same science has also made modern life so much easier and so much longer for so many. The universe, life, and especially human life give evidence of imperfections that cause oceans of suffering and death for God's creatures. The *problem of evil* seems to call into question that the universe is a product of divine love, and the misery and destruction we see all around lead many to reject the existence of God altogether. This is not a new problem, but modern science has made it even clearer by helping us understand the fragility of all life. In fact, destruction is written into the very fabric of the universe—our very sun is destined to fizzle out, along with the entire universe, which will expand until it is so spread out that it will whisper away. In addition, evolutionary biology and animal psychology have shown without a doubt that ruthless competitiveness and violence characterize the history of life. How can we reconcile the doctrine of God the Creator, God who is perfect Goodness and Love, with the presence of evil in creation? In the words of the English Dominican Herbert McCabe, "The world is full of suffering and sin; and God committed this world; he openly admits to having done so."[3]

So we must proceed, but we must do so with humility and caution. When we contemplate divine mysteries, two conditions of darkness can occur: mysteries above us that show reason's limits and contradictions below us that disturb and injure truth. We want the first, but not the second. If this chapter is successful, it will resolve some absurdities and contradictions, but will preserve mystery, because the real answer to the problem of evil is ineffable—it is hidden in the wounded heart of Christ, and it involves seeing the world in light of the Cross.

First I will try to adequately express the problem, relying on the thought of St. Augustine and others. This means facing a paradox: the paradox of divine creation and the existence of evil. Second, I will repeat and address one classic philosophical formulation of the problem, trying to reframe it in a way that offers the perspective of faith. Finally, I will return to Benedict's answer and share a true story that shows, in beauty but not in explanation, what the meaning of his answer looks like when it is lived.

THE CRY OF THE POOR

Let's start with a paradox, a tension that can never be resolved—all things, even our thoughts and own free actions, have both God for their source and also the capacity for evil. St. Paul, recognizing the imperfections of creation, speaks of the whole of creation groaning in pain (Rom 8:22). God, Creator and Source of existence for all things, made real the freedom of the Nazi concentration-camp guards, for instance, just as he made real the freedom of Mother Teresa as she gave herself to the poor of Calcutta.

Fifteen hundred years ago, St. Augustine expressed this paradox more poignantly than anyone, reflecting upon the evil he found in himself: "Who made me? Is not my God not only good but the supreme Good? Why then have I the power to will evil and to reject good? . . . Who put this power in me and implanted in me this seed of bitterness, when all of me was created by my very kind God?"[4]

Honest questions lead to insightful answers—it would be St. Augustine himself who would offer to history a clearer perspective on evil, often referred to rather unappealingly by philosophers as the *privation theory of evil*. He saw that evil was not a creature, for God cannot produce evil and, therefore, that it was not a subsistent reality, a "thing," of divine creation. Rather, evil is a lack or absence, the *privation*, of a good that should be present. Not all absences of good involve evil. A rock is not able to see, but we do not feel compassion for it as we do for a blind person or animal, because it is not in the nature of a mineral to see. Every created nature is limited; even when creatures have all the perfections that are natural to them—think of the acrobatics of purple martins— no creature has the infinite range of beauty, truth, and goodness that belong only to God, the Source of being to all things.

Interestingly, it was precisely the realization of God as Creator of all things that allowed Augustine to conclude that "there is no such entity in nature as evil."[5] Augustine's insight was formally proclaimed as a doctrine of the Catholic faith by the Council of Florence, right alongside its proclamation of creation *ex Trinitate*: "[This council] asserts that *there is no nature of evil* because every nature, in so far as it is a nature, is good."[6] The evil that causes

us to suffer and creation to groan is not a creature of God, not
something willed into being by him. It exists precisely when a
creature or (in the case of human beings) a thought, word, or free
action lacks something that it ought to possess by its nature. God
is not its source, although he does permit it.

We can distinguish two kinds of evil. The first kind, *physical
evil*, is evil that doesn't involve personal fault, although personal
fault is sometimes the cause of it. Physical blindness is an example—blindness is the nonexistence, the privation, of sight in a
creature whose nature it is to see. Many physical evils occur as
a matter of course because of physical good. Cancer happens
because mutations that drive evolution (which is good) also drive
disease (which is evil). Underwater earthquakes and their tsuna-
mis create human deaths and property destruction (evil) because
geological processes (good) that form beautiful tropical islands
(good) also deprive the earth's crust of stability, which causes evils
for creatures whose lives depend upon that stability.

The same is true with all biological life. As Aristotle keenly
observed, and any modern biologist can confirm, the generation of new life often requires *corruption*, which literally means
"destruction." The conception of a new human being requires the
corruption of the ovum and sperm, which cease to exist when
they combine to form the zygote. And in order to sustain their
lives, animals destroy other living things by consuming them,
hence the wise saying, "The life of the spider [good] is the death
[evil] of the fly."

Anytime we observe an example of physical evil and try to
identify it, we discover that it is impossible to "find" evil until
we come to some negative, some absence. The purely positive
properties of any existing thing cannot be called evil, even if those

positive properties are the cause of evil. As our recent international crisis has reminded us, a deadly *virus* consists of genetic material and a coating of protein. None of these positive components are evil; indeed, all living things are made up of genetic material and proteins. The evil of a deadly virus is not any part of it; rather, the *privation* of health and life it causes is the true evil. The coronavirus is not the evil; the absence of health and the negation of life it causes is the true evil. Therefore, the late Jesuit philosopher W. Norris Clarke called evil "a hole in being"; it is the lack of what ought to be present, the nonexistence of some good.[7]

The second and more tragic kind of evil Augustine identified as *moral evil*, evil in which rational creatures knowingly and freely deprive their own thoughts, words, and actions of the good that ought to be present within them. Once again, it is the "hole" within these that make them evil. Adultery is an example. Contrary to some well-meaning, but misinformed Christians, the evil of adultery does not consist in the bodily pleasure or personal intimacy involved in sexual intercourse, both of which are good in themselves in their proper context, which is marriage. The evil of adultery is the nonexistence of sexual fidelity when sexual fidelity ought to be present. This lack of loving fidelity to a spouse corrupts the good of adulterous sex from within, rendering it an inherently immoral, evil act. The evil of the crimes of the Nazis in the concentration camps involved the absence—in their thoughts, words, and deeds—of the proper respect for the human life and dignity of the Jewish people whom they imprisoned, tortured, and killed. The absence of compassion, respect for rights, kindness, and justice is what made Auschwitz evil, not the concrete walls of the gas chambers or the gases used for horrific purposes.

Finally, to call evil a privation is not to declare it to be non-existent or powerless. It is a lack where something truly ought to be present, and so it is always a privation, a hole, in something real. Because of this it is powerfully destructive simply by virtue of what it "takes away" and disfigures. Physical and moral evils are the source of all suffering for human beings, and those who suffer from these evils (and is there anyone who doesn't?) *really* do suffer, often in ways unimaginable to those who don't suffer to the same extent.

It is clear, then, that we have not resolved our paradox and the question that arises from it. Psalm 34:7 tells us that the "This poor one cried out and the LORD heard, and from all his distress he saved him." Our question is, If the Lord is the poor one's Creator, why must his creature need to cry out in the first place?

THE ANSWER OF CHRISTIAN FAITH

Why does God, the Source of all things, create a universe in which physical evil is actually a part of its functioning and in which moral evil permeates human life? The classic argument, proposed centuries ago by the English philosopher David Hume (1711–1776), runs as follows:

> God by nature must be both omnipotent (all-powerful) and omnibenevolent (all-good). Now if God is omnipotent, he *could* prevent all evil. And if he is all-good, he *would* do so, since it is the characteristic of a good person to prevent evil wherever possible. But in fact he does not prevent all evil, even though he could, but allows a vast amount of it, both physical and moral, as is evident in the world around us. Therefore, it follows

that God is either not omnipotent or not omnibenev-
olent. In either case such a being could not be God;
therefore, there is no God.[8]

It might help to place Hume and his argument in historical context. Hume was deeply influenced by a mechanistic conception of the universe, considering the universe as a massive
machine. And yet the great flaw of evil seems to him to undermine the idea of a divine mechanic. He looked for a God, omnipotent and omniscient, who created a flawless machine. But our
universe has many imperfections. For Hume, therefore, evil is
proof that this machine has no divine engineer behind it.

But engineers do not enter into personal relationships with
their creations. They love them as products, but not interperson-
ally. What if God created the universe for persons, out of love?
What if, as we will see in the coming chapters, God also allows
those persons to be real causes of one another? This changes the
picture radically. From this perspective, and above all from the
perspective of Christ's resurrection, which reveals what God *really*
wants for his creatures, we know that God gives freedom only for
the sake of goodness. The evil we see among other living creatures,
animals, who kill and rape ruthlessly, and above all in the dark
deeds of human beings, tells us that something has gone terribly
wrong, not due to God, but due to creatures—as we will see, due
to one creature in particular. When we look at the world through
the lens of Christ's resurrection, we can't say that evil is "just the
way things are," for we see there what God willed creation to be.

St. Paul speaks of how Christ reconciled "all things" to himself on the Cross (Col 1:20), not because nonhuman creatures
have done anything morally wrong, but because creation, invis-
ibly to us, has been wounded from the beginning by a terrible

wound. St. Paul VI captured this when, in 1972, he reminded the faithful of the abuse of freedom underlying the oceans of suffering that darken God's creation:

> What are the Church's greatest needs at the present time? Don't be surprised at Our answer and don't write it off as simplistic or even superstitious: one of the Church's greatest needs is to be defended against the evil we call the Devil.
>
> We find evil in the realm of nature, where so many of its expressions seem to speak to us of some sort of disorder. Then we find it among human beings, in the form of weakness, frailty, suffering, death and something worse: the tension between two laws—one reaching for the good, the other directed toward evil. . . .
>
> Evil is not merely an absence of something but an active force, a living, spiritual being that is perverted and that perverts others. It is a terrible reality, mysterious and frightening.[9]

Before we cry, "Aha! The devil made me do it!" remember that due to divine goodness, freedom goes all the way down. We ratify the rebellion of the devil and his fallen angels every time we sin.

From divine revelation we know a) that God creates out of perfect freedom for the sake of freedom, and b) that he creates the angels to freely participate in the development of his creation, and c) that some of them fell and mysteriously darkened creation in a way unintended by God. None of these truths of faith make any sense if the universe is just a machine, but then neither does the idea that human beings are free. There would be no human or angelic freedom in a mechanistic universe in which God prevented the possibility of all moral evil. In such a universe, human beings, acting morally with goodness as their goal, could accomplish no good freely as real causes of goodness. By preventing moral evil, God would also prevent us from collaborating with him in moral good. God would thus prevent fulfillment of his desire to perfect the world he created and to make moral masterpieces of our own lives, to love as he loves.

We do not want a divine dictator who would destroy our freedom; we want a heavenly Father who does not violate the universe and human freedom, a God who deals with us in love, not simply in power. This is what Pope Benedict was indicating in his inaugural homily by unmasking the unloving and totalitarian lie behind the false hope of a universe in which God prevents evil.

The answer of faith is the virtue of hope, the steadfast conviction that God *does* will a world without evil and is actively working to bring the universe and history to its perfect completion. In the words of 2 Peter 3:13, "But according to his promise we await new heavens and a new earth in which righteousness dwells." From this perspective, we can say to Hume: "Yes, God is all-good and all-powerful, and, yes, evil is present in a 'vast amount.' Therefore, God *will* defeat all evil." Indeed, God is already powerfully and mysteriously doing so by enabling his creatures to be themselves and by mercifully forgiving them when they fail. God works through holy men and women to transform the world through their free cooperation with him. God would not allow any evil unless he could and would bring some good from it.

This free cooperation and the transformation of the universe comes from the loving sacrifice that God took upon himself when he became a human being in order to accomplish our liberation from evil, sin, and death. First, Christ overcame moral evil in himself by being the perfect example of the fullness of human goodness with no moral evil whatsoever. In the words of sacred scripture, Jesus, the High Priest who offered himself in sacrifice for our sins, is not "unable to sympathize with our weaknesses, but . . . has similarly been tested in every way, yet without sin" (Heb 4:15). Second, in his sacrifice on the Cross Jesus overcame moral evil in all human beings by becoming an inexhaustible source of forgiveness to those who have sinned and becoming the one who reconciles all human beings to each other and to God. Finally, through the miracle of his resurrection, Christ overcame all physical evil and took our humanity into an indestructible life, preparing the coming of a new creation, a new heaven and earth, with no evil whatsoever. This is why St. Paul calls the risen Christ "the firstborn among many brothers" (Rom 8:29), because Christ offers us the way to join him, body and soul, in a universe to come that is perfectly fulfilled and transformed into the kingdom of God, and he offers us its seed and beginning in the community of the faithful, the Church.

THE CHRISTIAN REVOLUTION

But this unheard-of future is not something we can see with eyes unaided by faith, and it does not reduce the sting of the suffering evil causes. Evil will always be present in the world until the world is fulfilled in the New Creation. The way to endure evil, even to conquer it, is to walk daily with Christ crucified and risen, suffering patiently out of love and with others, helping the poor to carry their burdens, and recognizing that everyone's suffering is precious to God—not because he wishes us to suffer, but because love through suffering is divine and is a love that overcomes all evil. When we love God and love like God, our suffering in the face of evil is transformed into *sacrifice*, which is not misery, but a joy-filled hope that, in response to the cry of the poor, the Lord "will wipe every tear from their eyes, and there shall be no more death or mourning, wailing or pain, [for] the old order has passed away" (Rv 21:4). It is a confidence that in the New Creation, God will "be all in all" (1 Cor 15:28).

I want to end by offering an example of that kind of cruciform life, which hopes for the conquest of all evil but refuses to pretend that evil isn't there. It is the example of François Mauriac, the French Catholic novelist, in an encounter he had with a young journalist in 1954. The journalist had come from Tel Aviv to interview him on behalf of a daily newspaper. At first Mauriac was reluctant, but the journalist, he said, "won me over from the first moment." Mauriac opened up, and at one point he spontaneously shared about his wife's memory of cattle cars filled with Jewish children, noting that no one knew back then about the Nazi extermination methods. Mauriac exclaimed, "I have thought of these children so many times!" And the journalist said, "I was one of them." I have no words that can match Mauriac's response to this revelation, so I offer his:

> He was one of them! He had seen his mother, his
> beloved little sister, and most of his family, except his
> father and two other sisters, disappear in a furnace
> fueled by living creatures. . . .
>
> The child who tells us his story . . . was one of
> God's chosen. From the time he began to think, he
> lived only for God, studying the Talmud . . . wholly
> dedicated to the Almighty. Have we ever considered the
> consequence of a less visible, less striking abomination,

yet the worst of all, for those of us who have faith: the death of God in the soul of the child who suddenly faces absolute evil?

Let us try to imagine what goes on in his mind as his eyes watch rings of black smoke unfurling in the sky, smoke that emanates from the furnaces into which his little sister and his mother have been thrown after thousands of other victims: *Never shall I forget that night, the first night in camp, that turned my life into one long night seven times sealed. Never shall I forget that smoke. Never shall I forget the small faces of the children whose bodies I saw transformed into smoke under a silent sky. Never shall I forget those flames that consumed my faith forever. Never shall I forget that nocturnal silence that deprived me for all eternity of the desire to live. Never shall I forget those moments that murdered my God and my soul and turned my dreams to ashes. Never shall I forget those things, even were I condemned to live as long as God himself. Never.*

The name of the young journalist was Elie Wiesel, and thanks to the support of Mauriac, Wiesel's story—his memoirs of Auschwitz, which Wiesel entitled *Night*—would forever change the world's understanding of the Holocaust. *Night* is the story of the true, anguished cry of faith narrated as the loss of faith, like the outcry of Job that begins this chapter. Consider the darkest moment of the torment Wiesel suffered, as summarized by Mauriac: "When the child witnessed the hanging (yes!) of another child who, he tells us, had the face of a sad angel, he heard someone behind him groan: 'For God's sake, where is God?'" This is Wiesel's response: "And from within me I heard a voice answer: *'Where is he? This is where—hanging here from this gallows.'"* The hideous privation of that innocent child's life and dignity was a tiny "death" of God, for in that instance God's presence to the world was choked away. For where is his presence more keenly felt than in the innocence of a child?

I will not share any more of Wiesel's words. They must be read and contemplated in seriousness and in prayer and in weeping. But I do want to share Mauriac's response upon hearing the journalist's testament that day, because his response embodies the true Christian response to evil—the response that does not explain away the hideousness of evil but shows us the undying hope that God suffers with us and is on the side of the victim. This is the hope that God, who created all things, can and will and mysteriously already has defeated all evil, in the suffering of his Son, Jesus Christ, although we are not permitted to taste that victory in any way except in the trust of faith, the anticipation of hope, and the foretaste of self-giving love, mercy, and compassion. Here's Mauriac:

> And I, who believe that God is love, what answer was there to give my young interlocutor whose dark eyes still held the reflection of the angelic sadness that appeared one day on the face of a hanged child? What did I say to him? Did I speak to him of that other Jew, that crucified brother who perhaps resembled him and whose cross conquered the world? Did I explain to him that what would have been a stumbling block for *his* faith had become a cornerstone *for* mine? And that the connection between the cross and human suffering remains, in my view, the key to the unfathomable mystery in which the faith of his childhood was lost? . . .That is what I should have said to the Jewish child. But all I could do was embrace him and weep.[10]

And by embracing Wiesel, this great Christian said it all with his body, with his arms, with his sobs and his tears. He said more than words could say, and he has raised a question that I will not address here but to which I will return. And so I will say no more, but let scripture say the rest:

> Then I saw a new heaven and a new earth. The former heaven and the former earth had passed away, and the sea was no more. I also saw the holy city, a new Jerusalem, coming down out of heaven from God, prepared as a bride adorned for her husband. I heard a loud voice from the throne saying, "Behold, God's dwelling is with the human race. He will dwell with them and they will be his people and God himself will always be with them [as their God] . . . And he who sat upon the throne said, "Behold, I make all things new." (Rv 21:1–3,5)

3.

A FREELY EVOLVING UNIVERSE: GOD AND BIOLOGICAL EVOLUTION

There are no difficulties, from the viewpoint of the doctrine of the faith, in explaining the origin of man in regard to the body by means of the theory of evolution. . . . The doctrine of faith affirms that man's spiritual soul is created directly by God . . . the human soul, on which man's humanity definitively depends, cannot emerge from matter, since the soul is of a spiritual nature.

—St. John Paul II, General Audience, April 16, 1986

A LESSON FROM NARNIA

If it isn't apparent already, I am a fool for English writers regardless of creed, from atheists such as David Hume, Stephen Hawking, and Douglas Adams to believers such as G. K. Chesterton. But my first and still favorite English writer, the one whose work first tempted me to study theology as an undergraduate decades ago, is C. S. Lewis.

In chapter 1 we made a distinction between "how" and "why" explanations. In regard to "how" questions, the kind of questions that science answers, it is possible to get caught up in the amazing details of the universe and to fail to see beyond them to their deepest meaning. When we only have a grasp of the "how" and no notion of the "why," we cease to see reality for what it truly is, and we miss recognizing the deepest level of life's beauty and complexity. We see the history of the universe as only a sequence of events, not as the creation of our loving God who is, to all things, the Source and Summit of their beauty, goodness, and truth. Sometimes this happens because of our own failure to look closely enough. But when it comes to biological evolution, it can happen because of a failure to understand what we see. The details of biological evolution are surprising, not exactly what one might expect.

And this is where *The Silver Chair*, the fourth book of C. S. Lewis's famous children's series, The Chronicles of Narnia, offers us a great analogy. In the story, an English schoolgirl named Jill enters Narnia and is given a challenging quest: to rescue a prince who is being held captive by a magical and wicked enemy. To fulfill her quest she must recognize four signs that she will find in her adventure. Once each sign is encountered, she and her companions must faithfully perform certain actions.

As she stands on a mountain, looking down into Narnia, she is warned by Aslan, the loving creator and redeemer of Narnia, that the signs will not always be as obvious as they might seem. She is made to recite them, over and over, before she begins her quest. Then, once they are memorized, Aslan gives her the following counsel: "Here . . . I have spoken to you clearly: I will not often do so down in Narnia. Here on the mountain, the air is clear and your mind is clear; as you drop down into Narnia, the air will thicken. Take great care that it does not confuse your mind." Aslan completes his counsel with a warning: "And the Signs which you have learned here will not look at all as you expect them to look, when you meet them there. That is why it is so important to know them by heart and to pay no attention to appearances. Remember the Signs and believe the Signs."[1]

Jill begins her quest looking for the Signs but never with the care and attention they deserve. In fact, she and her friends either overlook or misinterpret the first three, and each time the quest suffers and almost fails. Only after repeated misadventures caused by misinterpretations of the Signs do she and her friends learn how to see them for what they are and not for what they expect them to be. They learn, through costly mistakes, to keep their eyes and their minds open. Slowly but surely they begin to understand the Signs, even while they overcome the hardships and dangers their mistakes brought upon them. When they reach the final Sign, their learning experiences make it possible for them to recognize it as such and to succeed at their attempt to rescue the captive prince.

The Silver Chair has an important moral for us and for everyone who wishes to understand the relationship between the doctrine of creation and science—specifically, the scientific consensus that all living things came into existence through biological evolution. In a real sense, many scientists and believers today are very much like Jill and her companions. We have been given very clear indications by God in sacred scripture and Catholic doctrine that he is the Creator of all things, including living things. Those living things, he tells us, are his creatures, willed by him and created by him. And yet, just as in Jill's case, the fact that the signs of God's creative activity do not appear as they were expected to appear prior to the discovery of evolution has created a challenge. We remember the signs, but do we still believe them? Or have we disbelieved or become confused because they now appear to us in ways that are different than we expected? To answer these questions, let's dispel some common misunderstandings of evolution, which are very common among creationists and cause them to feel their faith threatened by modern biology.

THE LICENSE PLATE GAME

When scientists talk about evolution, they also talk a lot about chance and randomness. Biologists explain the genetic variations that drive evolution as "random" occurrences. This is why the process of evolution is often presented as a blind, blundering, trial-and-error process. And from a purely scientific perspective, it is. The concern is whether this randomness somehow contradicts the teaching that an all-knowing God is governing the universe and that all things in it are part of a "divine plan," which is called divine providence. Many think that, if God is Lord of all of heaven and earth, then nothing could ever be called "chance."

The first step in overcoming this dilemma is recognizing that chance is in the eye of the beholder. Let's take a fun example. Some of you readers, like me, are so old that at one time in your childhood you had to go on at least one vacation without any technology to amuse you for the long car trip. You had nothing—no video players, no apps, not even a smartphone so you could text your friends about how bored you were. When we were kids we didn't just go to the mountains, we actually had to look at them!

In my family we would entertain ourselves by playing the license plate game. As we drove along, we would strain our eyes to see the license plates of the other cars on the road. Pulling into a busy McDonald's parking lot was a bonanza—fifteen to twenty cars all at once! Whoever was quick enough to yell out the state on a plate first got a point, and that state was taken off the list. Once we got to where we were going, whoever had the most points won. There were no prizes other than a chance to gloat.

What made the license plate game so much fun was that it was a game of chance. You never knew what plates you'd see; it was just whatever vehicles happened to be on the road. But does that mean that, for the drivers of those vehicles, they had no reason for being on the road? Of course not! Each of them had a purpose for whatever journey they were on. We didn't know their purpose, nor their itinerary, so we had no way to predict what plates we would see. It was truly chance for us, but it was not chance for them! If there was someone in the car who was all-knowing, who knew exactly where every car would be, then the chance element would be gone.

And there's our answer to this dilemma. Yes, the processes of evolution are chance from the scientific perspective. But for God, who knows everything, nothing is a matter of chance. That is why the book of Proverbs says, "Into the bag the lot is cast, but from the LORD comes every decision" (Prv 16:33). Accepting the presence of chance or random events in evolution, as well as in human life, is not a denial of God's providence. Even in the "accidental" elements involved in life, God is still the Lord of history and the universe.

For those who embrace an atheistic interpretation of evolution (aka evolutionism), the fact that evolution is random from our perspective means that evolution is random from *every* perspective; hence, there is no Creator. Such folks have obviously never played the license plate game!

St. Thomas Aquinas was on to this long before there were license plates. In his long treatise *Summa contra Gentiles,* there is a chapter (book 3, chapter 74) with the title "That divine Providence does not exclude fortune and chance," in which the great theologian argues exactly that. St. Augustine writes in his book *The City of God* that no one can in this life "escape being tossed about by chance and accident."[2] Scripture itself speaks of the role of chance in the world. In a very famous passage, the book of Ecclesiastes says, "Again I saw under the sun that the race is not won by the swift, nor the battle by the valiant, nor a livelihood by the wise, nor riches by the shrewd, nor favor by the experts; for a time of misfortune comes to all alike" (Eccl 9:11).

In summary, accepting the presence of chance or random events in evolution, as well as in human life, is not a denial of God's providence. Even in the "accidental" elements involved in life, God is still the Lord of both history and the universe.

INCREDIBLE CONVERGENCES

Before Darwin, when people assumed that each type of plant and animal had been directly crafted by the hand of God through "special creation," it was easier to say that living things, including ourselves, were "designed." Moreover, since God presumably had a reason for making each creature and for making it exactly the way it is, one could also easily say that each living thing had a "purpose." Darwin's theory seemed to undercut that way of thinking. Rather than being crafted directly by the hand of God, species were crafted by the blind and impersonal forces of random genetic mutations and natural selection. Both design and purpose seemed to go out the window.

But this is a misunderstanding. The fact that a process involves natural functions that have random outcomes in no way implies that it has no purpose. To help us understand this point, the philosopher Dennis Bonnette invites us to envision a roulette game.[3] The game of roulette depends on it being impossible for the players to predict exactly where the ball will land on any given spin of the roulette wheel. But this is not because the process, which involves chance, is without plan or purpose. In fact, everything is carefully orchestrated. The ball is given a round shape to allow it to bounce around the table. The wheel is carefully crafted so as to facilitate the bouncing of the ball at the beginning of the spin when the speed of the turning of the wheel is strongest and to facilitate the landing of the ball in a numbered slot when the speed slows to a certain point. The whole setup is designed to operate in a precise way, in accordance with the laws of physics. Not only would a physicist be able to explain in general terms how the roulette wheel functions, but he also would be able to tell you exactly where a particular ball would land if he were given the exact force of the spin, the exact dimensions of the ball, the diameter and shape of the wheel, and so on.

We see, then, a situation that involves at the same time both chance and purpose—and where, in fact, chance is involved in that purpose. The *purpose* is that of a certain kind of game. That game cannot be played unless *chance* is a part of it. (It is a "game of chance.") In order for the roulette wheel to produce the required "chance" or "random" events, it has to be *designed* in a certain way.

Interestingly, it seems as if modern science has begun to recognize that for evolution to occur at all, the universe must be structured in very specific ways that seem to reflect a divine purpose. In the last thirty years increasing attention has been paid by evolutionary biologists to the phenomenon called *evolutionary convergence*, "whereby unrelated [species] evolve nearly identical biological traits."[4] A classic example is the camera-type eye that has evolved independently in both humans and octopods. The human eye and the octopus eye have the same structures even though the evolutionary lineages of mammals and mollusks diverged before eyes evolved in either lineage.[5] Marsupial mammals in Australia and placental mammals in North and South America separated from some common ancestor more than one hundred million years ago. Yet on these two continents there has been the independent evolution of species with striking similarities: marsupial mice and placental mice, marsupial wolves and placental wolves, and so on.[6] The variation is minor compared to what they share. Most importantly, all of the major steps in the evolution of human beings—multicellularity, tissues, sensory systems, immune systems, eyes, limbs, and brains—are convergent: they evolved through many different pathways, but are found widely in unrelated species.[7]

In a series of important books, the Cambridge paleontologist Simon Conway Morris follows this trail of convergences to a remarkable conclusion: that the general forms that life can develop and adapt are not haphazard but follow definite chemical, genetic, and environmental pathways that were largely "predetermined from the Big Bang."[8] In other words, there is a deeper structure that makes the adventure of biological life not utterly random but orderly, somewhat like jazz music in which basic tunes (such as "When the Saints Go Marching In") are recognizable when played, but are always played with innovation and creativity, so that they are also a little different each time.

Morris compares the surprising precision of these evolutionary convergences to the discovery of Easter Island, the most remote speck of land in the earth's vastest ocean, by Polynesian seafarers fifteen hundred years ago. Superficially, one might guess this to have been an accident, a vessel blown off course and randomly drifting. But actually, clever Polynesian seafarers developed superb navigation techniques, discovering a way to quarter the ocean, widening their net of exploration until they covered it all and came upon Easter Island. In Morris's own words: "As with the audacious and intelligent Polynesians, so life shows a kind of homing instinct. . . . The net result is a genuine creation, almost unimaginably rich and beautiful, but one also with an underlying structure in which, given enough time, the inevitable must happen."[9]

The laws of physics and chemistry, therefore, seem not only fine-tuned to make life possible, but even fine-tuned to produce life. The universe, like the ancient Polynesian mariners, seems to have a kind of homing instinct for life's chemistry that is "built into" its chemical laws. There's nothing atheistic about that idea!

NATURE VS. CREATOR?

Finally, some people who reject or at least suspect evolution do so because it is *naturalistic*. Naturalism in its extreme form says that *only* natural explanations are valid. In other words, it denies any supernatural reality, which is wrong. But some people who oppose extreme naturalism go too far in the other direction. They think any attempt to find natural explanations is an attack on God. They think that the more we can explain "naturally," the less there is for God to do, and the less there is for which to praise God. For example, if it is said that an insect species arose by the natural processes of evolution, such people see this as a rival explanation to saying that God is the Creator of the world and everything in it. They imagine that we must then subtract the insect from the list of things that God created.

In other words, such people see nature and God as being in competition with each other. The more nature does, the less God is doing. Here our playwright analogy and our distinction between primary and secondary causality are very handy. If we say that a character in a play falls in love with another, this does not take anything away from the author of the play as an explanation of the events in the play. In fact, the more we understand what the characters are doing on their own terms, at the level of cause and effect *within* the play, the *more* we understand the mind of the playwright, and the more we know what he or she was up to in writing the play. The primary cause (the author) creates his story *through* the actions of the secondary causes (the characters). It makes no sense to ask, "Did Juliet accept Romeo's offer of marriage because Shakespeare wrote the play that way, or because she freely chose Romeo to be her husband?" These are two very different questions, and they must both be answered not only separately but also affirmatively. Shakespeare did not accept Romeo's offer of marriage; Juliet did so herself. But Shakespeare did conceive of Romeo and Juliet as well as their love for each other.

Of course, God can act directly without making use of secondary causes. He could create an insect species out of thin air.

However, God's use of natural causes, including "chance," reveals his power, intelligence, and skill in an even greater way than if he intervened miraculously to create them. Over one hundred years ago, an article in the famous *Catholic Encyclopedia* by a priest-scientist named Fr. Erich Wasmann captured this point, causing him to say that evolution is in "perfect agreement with the Christian conception of the universe": "If God produced the universe by a single creative act of his will, then its natural development by laws implanted in it by its Creator is to the greater glory of his divine power and wisdom. . . . Suárez [says], 'God does not interfere directly with the natural order where secondary causes suffice to produce the intended effect.'"[10] There is a natural order that comes from God, and the *greater* the powers and potentialities that God has implanted in nature, the *more* it shows forth his power and greatness.

Is evolution in contradiction to the doctrine of creation? Not if we are ready to see the signs of God's creative activity at work in it. In *The Silver Chair*, Jill did not expect her Signs to be strange; she thought they would turn up exactly as she expected. But we have it easier than Jill did, because something like evolution *was* expected, anticipated by the greatest theologian of the ancient Church, perhaps even the greatest theologian of all time—St. Augustine.

AUGUSTINE AND THE SEEDS OF LIFE

It can be fairly said that St. Augustine spent most of his adult life thinking about the book of Genesis. He wrote three different commentaries on Genesis. The first he found highly unsatisfactory; the second he disliked so much he didn't finish writing it.

Finally in AD 401 he began again, and fourteen years later he
completed his masterpiece, *De Genesi ad Litteram,* or *The Literal Meaning of Genesis.* By "literal" he meant, "according to the
intention of the human author."

Augustine's guiding principle of interpretation was reverence
for God's perfect wisdom. The First Creation Account narrates
God's creative activity over six twenty-four-hour days. But Augustine found the idea of separate creative acts on God's part to be
problematic when trying to explain the origins of living things,
even human beings. If God is perfect, his creative act must also
be perfect, lacking nothing, requiring no additional divine acts
to complete it. But he doesn't simply dismiss the text; because
it is inspired by God, he knows it must have some reason for
its details, and it is in inspecting those details that he makes an
amazing contribution to our journey of understanding creation.

One such detail is the significant difference he finds between
two ways that God's commands are depicted in Genesis 1. Sometimes God says, "Let there be"; other times God says, "Let the
earth bring forth." God uses the first kind of command to create
light (v. 3) and the firmament (v. 6) and to separate water from
land (v. 9). God uses the second kind of command to create living
things (as in v. 11 with vegetation and v. 24 with land animals);
the earth is "allowed" to bring them forth. Augustine concludes
that this second kind of command refers to things that are not
present in the world as actual beings, but as potentials of creation,
hidden within the elements themselves. The term Augustine uses
for these potentials is "rational seeds." His conclusion is that from
the first moment of time God made a universe naturally capable
of producing living things from nonliving matter when the conditions are right: "All these [living] things around us have been

seminally and primordially created in the very fabric, as it were, or texture of the elements; but they require the right occasion actually to emerge into being."[11]

Here we have a great Doctor of the Church saying that nature itself was the cause of living things, just as we see in evolution. But he doesn't stop with the plants and animals. In Genesis 1, God does not say, "Let the earth bring forth humans." But Genesis 2:7 does say that God formed man from the clay (literally: slime) of the earth. Therefore, Augustine concludes that human beings are no exception; the universe brings us forth naturally as well, calling us to be humble because of our earthly origins:

> Nor can it be said: "He himself made the man, while as for the beasts he gave the orders and they were made"... This same text, you see, which says that God molded the man from mud of the earth, also says that he molded the beasts of the field as well from the earth, when he led them to Adam . . . to see what he would call them. . . . So if he himself formed both the man from the earth and the beasts from the earth, what pre-eminence does the man enjoy in this respect?[12]

But this left him with a problem. Augustine knew that higher animals need parents to nurture them. So he wonders, "But in what manner did God make [the first human] from the mud of the earth? Was it straightaway as an adult, that is, as a young man . . . Or was it as he forms human beings from then until now in their mother's wombs?"[13] Augustine realized that it would be impossible for a first human to survive as a helpless infant without parents. This forces him to say that somehow it could be natural for "a young man in the prime of his life" to spring miraculously right from the clay—Adam! He realizes he is on shaky ground, so he immediately defends his answer that if it happened that way, it did not go "against nature except from our point of view . . . but not from God's."[14] Here St. Augustine has no recourse to any explanation to solve the dilemma that faces him.

If he had a solution, a way of proceeding that made sense, it would have allowed him to maintain fidelity to his central principle—namely, that God created the order of nature as complete from the beginning, with the potential to produce life without divine intervention. What Augustine needed to solve this riddle would be provided by another observer of nature, but it would be fifteen hundred years after Augustine died. Augustine could never have hypothesized common descent with modification through millions of years, because he had no idea of the age of the earth, which Darwin had discovered from geology. But a Catholic contemporary of Darwin, St. John Henry Newman, would see in Darwin a solution to Augustine's dilemma. In a deliciously sarcastic riposte to English churchmen of his day (and American creationists of our day) about Darwin's theory, he wrote:

> There is as much want of simplicity in the idea of the [miraculous] creation of distinct species as in that of the creation of trees in full growth, or of rocks with fossils in them. I mean that it is as strange that monkeys should be so like men, with no *historical* connection between them, as that there should be no course of facts by which fossil bones got into rocks. . . . I will either go the whole hog with Darwin, or, dispensing with time and history altogether, hold, not only the theory of distinct species but also of the creation of fossil-bearing rocks.[15]

Underlying St. Augustine's exegesis, and St. John Henry Newman's blessed sarcasm (ah, those English writers!), is an important theological principle. Both men saw God as not creating successively, as not deferring essential tasks until later, nor as needing to supplement the natural processes he set in place by way of miracles. St. Thomas Aquinas would agree that in the order of nature at its beginning, "we must not look for miracles, but for what is in accordance with nature."[16]

Of course, we must be modest regarding Augustine's interpretation. Some might fancy that Augustine advanced the theory of evolution fifteen hundred years before Darwin, but that would be claiming far too much. Darwin still gets credit for the theory of evolution. Augustine had no idea of *how* nature would go from nonliving to living, as we have seen. But from the theological perspective, his fascinating and careful reading of Genesis doesn't conflict with what we know now but fits it hand in glove. He saw it as strange to think of nature going from inanimate matter to full-grown complex animals. He was right. Yet he remained confident that the Creator would have a way to ensure that this would happen. He was right about that too. The Creator did have a way; modern science calls that way *evolution*.

Darwin and the whole field of evolutionary biology that he founded have helped us see that way; not a single step from mud to man, but modification through a long series of living ancestors. Without realizing it, Darwin went a long way toward securing the core theological principle behind Augustine's interpretation of Genesis.[17] And if Augustine could see a sign of God's creative wisdom in a natural origin to life, why shouldn't we accept evolution today?

In summary, it is safe to say that—on the basis of history, Church teaching, sound thinking, the example of great Christians, and our own theological reflection—faith can be found on the frontiers of evolutionary biology. As Fr. Wasmann recognized more than a century ago, Darwin's theory is in "perfect agreement" with the Christian conception of the universe, but the harmony between them can only be fully understood when approached through the eyes of faith.

CAN I GET AN "AMEN"?

Our Christian faith offers us a word that captures this co-creative relationship between God and creatures, a word used throughout the Christian liturgy and in personal prayer. It is the Hebrew word *amen*, a word that means "let it be" or "so be it." As the *Catechism of the Catholic Church* teaches, "*Amen* expresses solidity, trustworthiness, faithfulness." The *Catechism* goes on to explain that *amen* expresses "*both* God's faithfulness towards us *and* our trust in him."[18] The declared "amen," the "let it be," of believers is the expression of their willingness and openness to participate in God's plan.

Reading the First Creation Account in light of evolution reveals that even unconscious matter and nonrational living creatures display an "amen" in their acting according to their natures and capacity for action. Only when God says his own "Let there be," as he is portrayed doing throughout the First Creation Account, can creatures respond with the "So be it!" of their participation in God's plan. As Augustine saw, the biblical account of creation envisions the "both/and" of an originating, empowering "amen" of God and the responding, empowered, participating "amen" of the universe, its elements, and each level of creaturely existence.

As we imagine that chorus of creatures participating in God's creative activity, we might notice a unique set of voices among the barks, roars, hoots, and birdsong. As far as we know, only one of the many creatures we encounter throughout life's history on our planet can say "amen" to God in the same way that God says "amen" to creation. That is, only one of the creatures able to be studied by science can say "amen" to God with reason and freedom. The "amen" of creation would be missing its most perfect expression without the one creature who can express the "amen" offered by creation to God in the same "melody" with which God says it to the universe. That creature is the human person, created in the image of God. Our journey now brings us to the question of ourselves and the origins of our species.

4.

A COUPLE IN A CAVE? ADAM, EVE, AND THE ORIGINS OF HUMANITY

> The clay became man at that moment in which a being for the first time was capable of forming, however dimly, the thought "God." . . . The theory of evolution does not invalidate faith, nor does it corroborate it. But it does challenge faith to understand itself more profoundly and thus to help man to understand himself and to become increasingly what he is: the being who is supposed to say "thou" to God in eternity.
>
> —Joseph Ratzinger, *Dogma and Preaching*

ADAM, EVE, AND IMPERTINENCE

Children sometimes say the darndest things, and they are often very aware that science does too. My "darndest saying" was actually a science question, one I impertinently asked my mom in the drive-through of a bank when I was about seven years old. Most kids ask questions like, "Where do babies come from?"—but not me. As we waited for the clerk to put the canister back in the pneumatic tube (which seemed to me then, and even now, to be the very apex of technology), I dropped this one on her: "Mom,

61

if there was an Adam and Eve, what about Neanderthal Man?"
She gave me a surprised look, told me she'd have to think about
that, and then we drove away.

Forty-five years have come and gone, but my question is still
a hot topic for Catholics, and parents are just as stumped by it
today as they were back in the disco era. I know this because I am
asked similar questions whenever and wherever I speak on faith
and science topics, even when I am not addressing the theology
of human origins. Folks still find it tough to sort out the theology
of our salvation *prehistory*, even though we know so much more
now about the science than anyone did back when my mom had
no answer to give me.

In the early 1970s, it was thought that the Neanderthals
were our direct evolutionary ancestors. The genomes of both
our species and theirs have been thoroughly reconstructed by
some of the leading experts in the field, and thanks to their hard
work, we now know that our species, *Homo sapiens*, originat-
ed in Africa around three hundred thousand years ago, and the
Neanderthals emerged in Europe around four hundred thousand
years ago. Only later, in Europe or Asia, did the two species meet
up and interbreed—native Africans have no Neanderthal DNA,
but Europeans bear the telltale evidence of this interspecies han-
ky-panky, having anywhere from 1.8 percent to 4 percent of their
genetic code from our evolutionary cousins. When I asked my
darndest question, we had no idea about *Homo Denisova*, *Homo
floresiensis*, *Homo naledi*, and several other species whose fossils
have been discovered and who were also involved in the strange,
meandering path that led to you and me.

So geneticists, archaeologists, and paleontologists have
answered many questions about human origins from the scientific

point of view. We now have a lot more information about the hows, whens, and wheres of human evolution. But this has only made my youthful theological question, and others like it, more pressing. And as can be expected, some have pressed on to answers that simply do not agree fully with the scientific or the theological evidence, and many of the answers occupy that strange limbo between academic theology and public discourse: the energetic bloggers and YouTubers of the Catholic apologetics movement. Their answers all too often read like a thinly veiled cry for help.

This is not to reject apologetics, nor apologists. As scripture tells us, "Always be ready to give an explanation to anyone who asks you for a reason for your hope" (1 Pt 3:15), and apologists are like the Marines when it comes to being "always faithful" to this task. But I sometimes wonder if they have all the data, scientific and theological, that the task requires. It seems to me that many are trying to make the round peg of an ancient worldview fit the square hole of modern paleoanthropology, when perhaps there is a square peg available. For them, the solution to this puzzle at the heart of the encounter of faith and science is simple, even if defending it is complex. It all boils down to two—that is, two people: one man and one woman, Adam and Eve, what I like to call "The Couple in the Cave Hypothesis." But the problem is that science says this is a genetic impossibility. Given what is known about the human genome and its variations among humans living today, as well as the rate of genetic change and the genetics of our closest living animal relatives, the chimpanzees, there is no point in the six-million-year history of evolution leading to our species at which there could ever have been fewer than sixteen individuals.[1]

ADAM, EVE, AND OBEDIENCE

Let's consider an example of one attempt to reconcile science and theology at the origins of humanity that I have chosen precisely because I am impressed by its serious thoughtfulness. In summer 2019, an anonymous blogger (pseudonym "ACTS Apologist") claimed the following: "The Christian faith is sometimes called a 'historical religion.' This means it isn't just a philosophy of life. It makes claims about world history, claims which need to be true for its teachings to have *any merit*. Among these are . . . a real Adam and Eve."[2]

The ACTS Apologist then goes on rightfully to reject a common "urban legend" propagated by many apologists—that two of our ancestors, whom geneticists call mitochondrial-Eve and chromosomal-Adam, were the only first humans, and that we know that they mated with each other.[3] He also correctly acknowledges that there were "non-rational biological humans (NRBH's)" around at the time of our origins. We know from the fossil record that for as long as three hundred thousand years, ancestors of all humans today had our anatomy, but didn't think or act like us. They had no capacity for objectivity, which as far as we know distinguishes us from every other creature on our planet, and so no art, no religion, no books for Ave Maria Press!

But then he tries to cross a bridge too far:

> Let's suppose that roughly 80,000 years ago, God reached into a community of NRBH's in the African continent and granted two individuals the gift of a rational soul. This could be accompanied by a physical (genetic) change, or even an epigentic [*sic*: epigenetic] change—either way.

> Those two humans were offered a life at peace with God, but reject[ed] it. They eventually have children. Some of these kids might have mated with each other. Others might have mated with the NRBH's which surrounded them. And when they did, their children had the nature of the "true" human parent, with the "rationality switch" kicked on.[4]

Here the ACTS Apologist misunderstands what the Catholic tradition means by a "rational soul." It is not something that comes from outside of us. It is essential to us, forming one "me" along with my body, which is the other component principle that makes a human being. To grant a rational soul to an already living "NRBH" would violate its very identity—the RBH after would have no true continuity with the NRBH that came before, a sort of prehistoric soul-swapping as in Disney's *The Princess and the Frog*. (By the way, this is also why it is incorrect to speak of priestly ordination as a substantial change, as some well-meaning folks innocently do.) The Church does teach that the soul is the product of special divine creation, a Catholic doctrine that I'll discuss more later in this chapter. But to reach down and grant a soul to an already living being makes no sense if the soul is the form of a body—that which makes a human being a living body versus a corpse. This is difficult to understand, I know, but essential to Catholic teaching, having been formally defined by an ecumenical council, the Council of Vienne, in 1311–1312.

In his defense, the ACTS Apologist makes this move because he feels beholden to Church teaching, as he notes at the beginning of his post. And the teaching he cites is closely related to why far too many Catholic apologists make so many questionable leaps of logic. That teaching seems to answer in the negative the question "Can one be a faithful, obedient Catholic and accept more than two rational biological humans at the beginning of the human race?" Before we move on to the question of the creation of the human soul, and what makes our life principle so special, we must first squarely face this question.

Let's consider the teaching itself, which can be found in the 1950 encyclical by Pope Pius XII called *Humani generis*, "Concerning Some False Opinions Threatening to Undermine the Foundations of Catholic Doctrine." Pius was concerned that a movement in Catholic theology at the time, called the Nouvelle Théologie, might undermine the Church's emphasis on the theology of St. Thomas Aquinas. Less than a decade and a half later, however, Nouvelle theologians such as Jean Danielou, Hans Urs von Balthasar, Yves Congar, Henri de Lubac, and a young Joseph Ratzinger would be luminary experts at the Second Vatican Council, loved and esteemed by John XXIII, Paul VI, and the majority of the bishops who served as council fathers. But at the time of his encyclical, the movement raised concerns that Pius XII, fulfilling his sacred duty, judged necessary to address.

Toward the end of the encyclical he raised matters pertaining to the harmony of faith and science. He began by opening the door, for the first time in an official Church document, to the science of biological evolution, even the evolution of the human body, allowing "research and discussions, on the part of men experienced in both fields [science and theology]," on this matter. But then he put the brakes on one possible direction this discussion might take, using the term *polygenism*, which he defines in this passage:

> When, however, there is a question of another con-
> jectural opinion, namely polygenism, the children of

the Church by no means enjoy such liberty. For the faithful cannot embrace that opinion which maintains that either after Adam there existed on this earth true men who did not take their origin through natural generation from him as from the first parent of all, or that Adam represents a certain number of first parents. Now it is in no way apparent how such an opinion can be reconciled with that which the sources of revealed truth and the documents of the Teaching Authority of the Church propose with regard to original sin, which proceeds from a sin actually committed by an individual Adam and which, through generation, is passed on to all and is in everyone as his own.[5]

Now the ACTS Apologist is right to take this seriously—it is a papal statement on a matter of faith. But his truth trajectory starts to disintegrate when he claims that a "real Adam and Eve" is a claim necessary for the teaching of the Church to have "any merit." There are two important reasons why this teaching of Pius XII could not have such far-reaching significance.

First, *Humani generis* is an encyclical, not an infallible definition. For an example of an infallible definition, we need look no further than Pius XII's definition of the bodily Assumption of the Blessed Virgin Mary, which he defined in the apostolic constitution *Munificentissimus Deus* just two and a half months after he promulgated *Humani generis*. As Vatican II makes clear, Catholics must give the firm "submission of faith" to matters that have been infallibly defined (certainly the case in regard to the Assumption) and "a religious submission of mind and will" to the ordinary papal magisterium (certainly exercised by Pius XII in *Humani generis*). [6] This is not a meaningless distinction—the "obedience of faith" is about something that must be believed with the same commitment that we believe in all of the articles of the Creed. But the "religious submission of mind and will" falls short of the absolute and irrevocable assent that the first kind of teaching requires. It can be fulfilled, in the words of the late theologian Francis Sullivan, by "an honest and sustained effort to achieve internal assent to [a] teaching." One's response is valid even when internal assent cannot be achieved due to weighty objections, as long as this is one's stance only in exceptional circumstances,[7] such as when the progress of science requires us to seriously reconsider our long-standing assumptions about how and when the first humans came to be and even how many first humans there were. (By the way, "weighty objections" do not include personal taste, or keeping up with political or societal fads, or just a lack of desire to assent—just sayin'.)

But even if, for the sake of speculation, we imagined that *Humani generis* contained an exercise of papal infallibility, Pius XII's own words would clearly indicate that the paragraph in question was not where that exercise occurred. He was very careful in his wording. He said that "it is in no way apparent" how polygenism can be squared with the doctrine of original sin. He could have said "it cannot be reconciled" with definitive Catholic teaching, but he did not. He was clearly being cautious and leaving the door open for possible scientific discoveries that might generate some theory of polygenism that could be harmonized with what we know by faith: that original sin is passed on to all human beings due to a real human sin committed at the dawn of human history. In a recent trip to Rome to study the drafts of *Humani generis*, the American Catholic philosopher Kenneth Kemp was able to confirm that, in the early drafts, the language here is categorical, stating that polygenism absolutely cannot be reconciled with the doctrine of original sin. But as the drafts progress, the language changes.[8] So thanks to this careful investigator, we now know that putting the emphasis on "not apparent" is accurate.

Joseph Ratzinger had already realized in 1964 that flexibility was possible (and now we know, necessary) to move beyond a solitary couple, Adam and Eve. In a classroom lecture, he noted that the doctrine of original sin was not about head-counting the first humans: "The purpose of the doctrine of the original state *is not to recount a piece of empirical history* and thus to expand our knowledge of history into the prehistoric."[9] He would make the same point to the entire Church as Pope Benedict XVI in his 2011 Easter Vigil homily, saying then that the biblical creation accounts are "not information about the external processes by which the cosmos and man himself came into being."[10] If we are looking for paleoanthropology in the pages of the Bible, we will not find it, nor should we expect to. After all, the Hebrew word *āḏām* (Adam) means "humanity," and the Hebrew word *ava* (Eve) means "life," "to give life." And when you have a narrative in which *humanity* marries *life*, who gives birth to all the living, you are dealing with something so much more important than science—you are dealing with a symbolic account of the creation of humanity that points to the deepest meaning of things.

Pius XII did say something perennial, however, on the matter of human origins in *Humani generis* that would be repeated by St. John Paul II, and which needs more explaining. I have already mentioned it—the special creation of the human soul. Properly understood, this important doctrine is a matter of faith, and it is the foundation of human dignity. But as we shall see, it is not a matter of God reaching down, working his way around the

biology of being human, but instead of God reaching through it
in order to lovingly fashion in his image each and every human
being.

THE BOOK OF GENESIS AND THE HUMAN SOUL

The Second Creation Account in the book of Genesis (1:4b–2:3)
narrates the creation of human beings in one verse, Genesis 2:7:
"The LORD God formed the man [Hebrew: *ādām*] out of the dust
of the ground [Hebrew: *ādāmah*] and blew into his nostrils the
breath of life, and the man became a living being." The connection between the word for "ground" (*ādāmah*) and the word for
"human being" (*ādām*) shows that humans are naturally made
of physical elements. It is a humbling image, one that is wide
enough to include the discovery of a long, natural evolution from
earlier living creatures in which matter, the stuff of the ground,
is ultimately fashioned into humanity, the image of God. Based
on this theological truth, which harmonizes so beautifully with
the truth about human origins, no one of us can say, "My race is
somehow better than all others." In the words of Pope Benedict
XVI, "Despite every distinction that culture and history have
brought about, it is still true that we are, in the last resort, the
same . . . earth, formed from dust, and destined to return to
it. . . . The Bible says a decisive 'No' to all racism and to every
human division."[11]

Just as the First Creation Account was responding to and
correcting the violent, dehumanizing worldview of the Babylonian myth *Enûma Eliš*, Genesis 2 responds to yet another Ancient
Near Eastern myth, the *Atrahasis* (named after its main character),

which was first written down sometime around 1700 BC. In this myth, humanity is created by Enki, the god of wisdom, to be the slaves of the gods. Clay and the blood of a slain god are mixed together, and all the gods spit upon the mixture. After ten months seven male and seven female human beings are produced, beginning the human race.

The Second Creation Account, which is best understood as a symbolic account of human origins, has some interesting similarities with this pagan myth. Just as in the *Atrahasis,* humans are made out of clay in the Second Creation Account. But unlike the *Atrahasis*, God doesn't spit, but rather breathes into the human being his own "breath." This is what sets humans apart from the other animals, who also have the breath of life (see Genesis 6:17), but not as breathed directly from God. This Second Creation Account describes an animal that has a life more like God's than the rest of the animals, who is not simply one of God's creatures but who becomes a "living being" precisely because of a special relationship to him. The Hebrew word for "being" in Genesis 2:7 is *nephesh*, a word that can be translated as "soul" or "life principle." Thanks to God's mysterious action, a living human being exists.

The issue of the origin of the human soul is the one issue about which the Church has qualified her openness to what science has revealed about our evolutionary origins. To quote St. John Paul II, "The doctrine of faith affirms that man's spiritual soul is created directly by God . . . the human soul, on which man's humanity definitively depends, cannot emerge from matter, since the soul is of a spiritual nature."[12] So from the theological perspective, the "human difference" is located in the fact that the soul is spiritual and directly created by God; it is not merely the result of a biological process. In fact, this is the case for every human being; whenever a new human being is conceived, it must involve God's direct creation of the soul of that human being.

How does God "directly create" a human soul? In our ordinary way of thinking, it is easy to imagine that whenever a human body is "made," God makes a soul for this body, "attaching" the two. Many mistakenly think of themselves as *two* things, a living body and a mysterious ghost that is the real self. This, however, is to misunderstand the nature of the soul, which is not a separate thing that God makes but, along with the matter from which our body is made, is one of two principles that make a human being a living being. No part of us is simply soul; no part of us is merely body. In fact, a human body without a soul is not a body at all. As the soul is the very life principle of a living body, a body without a soul is only a corpse.

At the beginning of our species, and indeed at the beginning of every human life, we have a paradox. From one perspective, human beings are the natural product of primate evolution, the end-result of a meandering process that involves trends we see in our evolutionary ancestors: bigger brains, more sophisticated tools and social organization, and so on. From the deeper perspective, each human being is a rational and spiritual being, the product of God's loving initiative that engages each of us in a special relationship with our Creator. The International Theological Commission (ITC) expresses the mystery of the *direct* (also called *special*) *creation* of the human soul in a way that sheds light on this paradox: God can "bring about effects that transcend the capacity of created causes acting according to their natures" in which God directly causes the soul in a "non-disruptive" way.[13] Human souls, then, do come from parents; through the fertilization of the female ovum by the male sperm, human parents are the created causes acting according to their sexual natures. What makes human reproduction different is not that God disrupts it, but rather that God causes it to produce a life principle that transcends that of the other animals. As the absolute ground of being, God causes *within* the causing of the parents, allowing them to transcend themselves *in their own act of causing*.

Therefore, the direct creation of the human soul is not to be understood as a miracle, at least not in the strict theological sense (in the poetic sense, of course it is, and always!). Miracles are singular, one-time events, such as the raising of Lazarus from the dead (see John 11:1–44), but the direct creation of the human soul happens whenever human sexual reproduction is successful in the normal course of nature. Yet it is more like a miracle than other natural events because here, as in the case of miracles, natural causes are empowered to produce something beyond their capacity.

Now we have the background to understand that the special creation of the human soul is not God pushing creation buttons or interfering with nature, but God bringing it beyond itself to its greatest height—human life. As Pope Benedict XVI explained,

> If creation means dependence of being, then special creation is nothing other than special dependence of being. The statement that man is created in a more specific, more direct way by God than other things in nature, when expressed somewhat less metaphorically, means simply this: that man is willed by God in a specific way, not merely as a being that "is there," but as a being that knows him; not only as a construct that he

> thought up, but as an existence that can think about
> him in return. We call the fact that man is specifically
> willed and known by God his special creation.[14]

In summary, the human soul, the very life principle that makes a human body to be a living body of a specific kind, is not a thing God makes separately. Rather, due to the free unfolding of a universe that he sustains in being precisely for this purpose, a body of the human kind is, of its essence, a body that must have a spiritual soul to be the kind of creature that it is. The spiritual soul is the principle that, with the body, makes a human being a living being. Evolution, according to the God-given laws of the universe and due to the activity of creatures over millions of years, has yielded a situation where in our universe there is now a material creature for whom to be spiritual is its natural state, whose origins implicate God and require his direct involvement.

This mystery reveals a truth that science could never discover but that faith and reason together can discern: *Homo sapiens* is the ultimate reason for why the universe exists, the point of God's creative activity. From all eternity God did not merely share his goodness with creatures, but he willed for there to be a creature that could knowingly and freely receive the gift of the created universe and, ultimately, the gift of his own divine life. As St. John Paul II taught,

> Creation is a gift because man appears in it, who, as an
> "image of God," is able to understand the very meaning
> of the gift in God's call from nothing to existence. . . .
> Man appears in creation as the one who received the
> world as a gift, and vice versa, one can also say that the
> world has received man as a gift.[15]

The created universe could not be a gift unless there was a creature who, being capable of understanding, could wonder at its beauty, respond to it with delight, and begin to comprehend its patterns and laws with gratitude toward the Creator. The human difference—and the paradox of special creation—lies precisely in this uniquely human capacity, which places us in an intimate relationship with the Trinity, who calls us into being out of nothingness and then calls out to us in love.[16]

SO LONG AGO THE GARDEN

God calls humanity out of nothingness through the divine act of creation and through the union of man and woman, a perfect concourse of divine and creaturely activity. He then calls out to humanity in love. But here we must pause, because each of us knows a dirty little secret—that we rarely if ever respond to that call, that it falls again and again on deaf ears. Sometimes, human beings seem fine-tuned for evil, not for good, as our able guide Joseph Ratzinger has also noticed. "Man is God's image—and only man," he taught, and then he gave us the bad news:

> When we reflect more deeply on this, we can be assailed by a dreadful feeling. There are, indeed, many blessed moments in which something of God becomes visible through man: in the great works of art that have been given to man in his history, we sense something of God's creative imagination, something of the Creator Spirit and of his eternal beauty that transcends every word and all the calculations of logic. . . . But our experience is much more strongly marked by the opposite. In his history, man so often seems to prove the existence of a

demon (or at least of an ambiguous being) rather than
of a good God. Man disproves the existence of the God
to whom the creation points. . . . We need not recall
such terrible names as Nero, Hitler, or Stalin; it suffices
to think of our own experiences with other people and
with our own selves.[17]

We have met the enemy, and he is us. It is to this sad problem
of human life, called sin and moral evil, and its mind-blowing
resolution to which we now turn.

5.

FROM BLOMBOS CAVE TO BETHLEHEM: SCIENCE, SIN, AND THE SACRED HEART

> If only there were evil people somewhere insidiously committing evil deeds, and it were necessary only to separate them from the rest of us and destroy them. But the line dividing good and evil cuts through the heart of every human being. And who is willing to destroy a piece of his own heart?
>
> —Alexander Solzhenitsyn, *Gulag Archipelago* (1973)

PEERING INTO THE PAST

In 2002, a discovery was made in a South African cave that is widely regarded as one of the most important finds of all time for understanding the "when" and "where" of human beginnings, the advent of our species. Two pieces of engraved ochre, dating back seventy-five to one hundred thousand years ago, were discovered bearing cross-hatch patterns with parallel incised lines.[1] They are the oldest known examples of human artifacts that can be confidently interpreted as symbolic. What seems clear is that the humans at Blombos Cave existed on our side of a cognitive breakthrough—the emergence of symbolic thought, the ability to organize the world around us mentally by generating a vast array of symbols in which one thing stands for something else.[2]

Symbolism is at the heart of the difference between animal communication such as birdsong and human language, between skillful problem solving and reflection upon the intrinsic nature of things, between personal ornamentation and artistic expression, between intelligence and reason. Other animals act intelligently and make natural judgments, but we human animals have the *power of reason,* the power to transcend mere appearances and to get at how things are in themselves. In other words, humans are able to pursue and know truth—and it may have been in a place like Blombos Cave that the first glimmerings of human reason appeared.

And yet this exciting discovery is troubled by yet another—the cooked remains of a cannibal feast from the same region.[3] The early humans at Blombos Cave or others like them, indeed like us, were capable of dark deeds. Human inclinations, desires, and instincts, then as now, are riddles, pointing in opposing directions. St. Paul captured this tragic paradox perfectly as he lamented his own life experience in his Letter to the Romans: "What I do, I do not understand. For I do not do what I want, but I do what I hate. . . . The willing is ready at hand, but doing the good is not. For I do not do the good I want, but I do the evil I do not want" (7:15, 18–19).

In this chapter we will investigate the ways in which science, philosophy, and faith can together deepen our understanding of this tragic element of human nature and history: the pervasiveness of sin and moral evil. Using the examples of blind ideologies and racism, we will explore how so many of the worst human tendencies have been illuminated by modern cognitive science, which shows that the animal nature we inherit from evolution is at the root of our tendencies toward both moral goodness and moral evil. We will explore how the Christian tradition has recognized this and what it tells us about God's original plan for humanity, which was postponed—but not terminated—by original sin. Sinfulness is often wrongly considered to be what Christianity is all about, as if our salvation is primarily about blame or condemnation. On the contrary, the center of the Gospel is God's love for humanity made flesh in Jesus Christ; the topic of sin reveals our need for redemption so that we might fully receive that love, which we will also explore.

To begin, let's explore two examples that highlight the dilemma of being human.

THIS POOR HEART OF MINE

In human history great ideas have often mutated into poisonous and even murderous ideologies in which a partial explanation is taken as the *only* explanation for just about everything. In the early twentieth century, as Darwin's brilliant discovery of natural selection began to be more fully appreciated, it just as quickly began to be wrongly applied to human life and society. In this misinterpretation of Darwin's theory, called *social Darwinism*, it became the responsibility of governments to play the role of the environment, to "aid" natural selection by controlling human "breeding" (called *eugenics*) and even sterilizing those considered physically or mentally deficient. In *Buck v. Bell*, a 1927 U.S. Supreme Court ruling, the door was opened nationally for compulsory sterilization of the unfit, including the mentally handicapped, "for the protection and health of the state"; this was an attempt to improve the human race by eliminating "defectives" from the gene pool.[4] Across the Atlantic, in Nazi Germany, social Darwinism was behind one of the most horrific events in human history—the unspeakable evil of the Holocaust.

Social Darwinism fueled movements of white supremacy and gave them a pseudo-scientific justification. It legitimized various expressions of racism, which has been condemned by the Church as "a violation of human dignity and a sin against justice."[5] In the name of the pseudo-science of social Darwinism, the racist lies of white superiority and even of a "master race" flourished and found expression in widespread violence and discrimination.

The great irony is that racism has been largely undermined by modern genetics. It turns out that all human beings are 99.9% genetically the same and that the differences between races and ethnicities are vanishingly tiny. A study conducted in the early part of the last decade tested the DNA of 1,056 people from fifty-two populations in five major geographic regions of the world: Africa, Eurasia (Europe, the Middle East, Central and South Asia), East Asia, Oceania, and the Americas. Of the tiny 0.1% difference in DNA, 94% is among individuals of the same populations, and only 6% is between individuals from different populations.[6] By comparison, a single population of chimpanzees in West Africa is said to have more diversity in its DNA than the entire human population has today![7] Skin color, which has been and remains a source of social division and an ocean of misery, violence, and misunderstanding throughout history, turns out to be a micro-adaptation to various climates that has actually been independently acquired numerous times by human populations living in various regions of the world.

Racism, then, has no foundation, scientific or otherwise. And yet, its dark legacy continues and is alive and well today, as we sadly know all too well. It is only one example of the numerous ways in which fear, discrimination, and even murderous violence against those considered different and inferior have cast shadows over virtually every human society. Innocent blood spilled over differences of skin color, culture, and religion runs like a river through human history. From where do such evils come?

Placing the poisonous ideology of social Darwinism side by side with violence against those different from us can answer that pressing question. With respect to blind ideologies like social Darwinism, it seems that the repetition of false claims, even claims that are known to be false, has the effect of making them seem more truthful to those who encounter them.[8] The human brain favors statements that have already been processed, which can create a situation in which groups large and small become blinded by falsehoods. Such "thinking shortcuts," also known as *cognitive biases*, tend to limit our openness to new ways of thinking, even when our standard ways of thinking are absurd.[9] And yet, this very tendency is one that also makes us capable of trusting all kinds of genuine sources of knowledge, such as pastors, friends, and family, upon whom we rely for 99 percent of the information that we have and the truths that we know. What can lead in some cases to the spread of ideologies like social Darwinism is also essential to knowing the truth and living in society.

Moving to the evil of racial and ethnic discrimination, other research shows that we have a natural tendency "to make distinctions between 'us' and 'them.'" As social animals that live in groups, we have an innate tendency to favor members of the "ingroup" and to be less inclined toward trusting members of "outgroups." Similar behaviors have been detected in other primates, which indicates that the roots of *outgroup bias* reach far back into our evolutionary history. And yet, the same tendency is also behind our inclination to bond into groups and to offer mutual support to each other within them.[10]

Do trust and ideology, group bonding and racism, and good and evil go hand in hand? How do we explain the "dividing line" between them that runs through our hearts? Evolutionary psychology has a lot to offer to answer this question from the "how" perspective. Cell biologist Kenneth Miller concludes, based on studies of the architecture of the human brain: "The circuitry of the brain is in fact a poorly integrated mixture of the truly ancient, the very old, and the relatively new all working side-by-side."[11]

Despite being one of the great wonders that evolution produced, our biological and neurological inheritance has its shortcomings. This fact explains a great deal about *how* humans so often act irrationally and contrary to goodness, including why racism and other forms of bias seem to crop up throughout society and history, why male human beings find it so hard to treat women as equals and not as objects, and why wars and the killing of the innocent are constants in human history. There is nothing from the scientific perspective that should make us surprised by this. Yet what makes sense from the "how" perspective of human evolutionary science falls short of the "why" perspective of theology, which looks at human life from the perspective of human happiness and God's intentions for the human family. We yearn for better than what evolution could give us, and thanks to the

Christian faith, we know that what evolution produced was not the finished product.

THE ANIMAL WITHIN

In chapter 2 we encountered the problem of evil. We saw that evil is a privation, the absence of a good that ought to be present. We also observed that most physical evils occur as a matter of course because of physical good. "The life of the spider is the death of the fly"; physical evil is so deeply intertwined with physical good that they are impossible to separate. At the same time, we know that, even though we are rational, we are also animals whose brains are physical organs that are necessary for our exercise of reason in this life. So, our brains share the same ambiguity as the rest of physical reality. We have instincts and inclinations that can be interpreted as evil from one angle, but never from *every* angle. In fact, it is possible for human beings to come to understand their instincts and inclinations and to consciously choose between them: to treat those different than us as if they were beloved blood relatives, to confront with logic and truth the false ideologies that threaten to sway our minds toward darkness, and to discipline urges that are contrary to goodness.

The insight that our physical bodies bear the same ambiguities as all animals is not new. In his greatest theological work, the *Summa Theologiae*, St. Thomas Aquinas observed this strange paradox. On the one hand, he observed, we have been made for perpetual, everlasting happiness, something we are capable of thanks to being created in the divine image, endowed with reason and freedom. However, when he considered our nature from the perspective of our biological makeup, he observed that the human body is not perfectly adapted to our spiritual capacities. Nature, he speculated, gave the best it was capable of, producing a body with features that are useful for rational animals (such as sense and touch; today we would add a sophisticated frontal cortex). But much like a blacksmith might choose iron to make a knife for one set of reasons (iron is hard, for example, and can be made very sharp), he might also regret that same material for other reasons, such as the tendency of iron to rust easily.[12]

And as it is with the blacksmith's use of iron to make a knife, so it is with human beings, creatures made in the image of God who are also the products of evolution. We have the proper kind of biological makeup for a rational animal, but due to the limitations of the material world, this makeup cannot in itself provide us with everything humans need to be the perfect embodied image of God. God is Truth and Love, but our reason and freedom are constantly interacting with our animal instincts and inclinations, and these are not always easy to harmonize with knowing the truth and loving freely. Thanks to the gift of reason, we are capable of understanding what intellectual, moral, and physical excellence entails. Yet we so often cannot be our "best selves," but choose, rather, to do what we know we ought not to do.

It is utterly incorrect, however, to conclude that what we received from evolution has made us intrinsically evil. It has made us only what any biological process can produce: a creature that pursues survival, physical health, sensual pleasure, and other goods. These are sufficient for an animal existence, and even the bad tendencies we discover in ourselves arise only in relation to the goods that we strive for by nature. But through the gift of the rational soul, as St. Thomas also knew, God made us capable of knowing the difference between right and wrong, of being able to make judgments about our judgments.[13] In addition, the Christian perspective of God's intention for humanity offered St. Thomas an insight that science and philosophy, left to themselves, could not provide.

OUT OF EDEN

In recognition of the divine purpose of moral perfection and perfect happiness for which God created human beings, St. Thomas concluded that God not only created us in a special dependence upon him, but that he also endowed our first parents with special gifts that go beyond what they could have received from the material world and our animal nature. Through a supernatural grace given to the soul, the body would have been preserved from all corruption and from death,[14] bodily desires and emotions would have been wholly subject to reason,[15] and a life lived in untainted goodness and happiness, in unbroken communion with God, would have been the result. These special endowments, called the *preternatural gifts* (literally gifts "other than nature"), were not part of our biology. God wished to give us graces to perfect our natural state, making it correspond to his ultimate intentions for us. St. Thomas also speaks of the gift of *original integrity* as that by which God assisted our first parents to overcome their tendency toward a conflict between knowing, choosing, and desiring, what paleoanthropologist Ian Tattersall calls our "apparently contradictory cognitive condition."[16] Assumed here by St. Thomas is that, as animals, we are not able to easily integrate our reason and freedom with our desires; as composite beings, we tend over time toward physical disintegration, not integration. Taken together,

these graces with which God endowed our first parents empowered them to readily realize the best possibilities provided to them
by the "human difference."

When trying to conceive of what such an existence would
have been like, our imaginations can tend to run away with us
to fanciful places. Some think of the first humans living in an
earthly paradise in which our planet, or at least some region of
it, was radically different than it is now, a place where nothing
ever died and in which no physical evils were present. But it is
more helpful to think of "paradise" as the privileged way in which
sinless humans would have existed in this world *as it is*, or at least
as it was. Others assume that freedom from death would have
meant a perpetual lifetime for humans on earth. However, St.
Augustine taught that eventually our first parents and their sinless
descendants would have entered into a glorified state comparable
to the risen Christ. Still others assume that freedom from suffering would have meant freedom from any pain whatsoever and a
situation in which humans would not need to strive or mature
in wisdom and virtue. But this also has never been the teaching
of the Catholic Church.[17]

We do not know how long the first humans remained in a
sinless state. Original integrity and these special gifts may very
well have been lost as quickly as they were received, or perhaps
they remained for a day, a week, or a year. Some theologians
speculate that the first humans never actualized these gifts before
they sinned. In 1964, Ratzinger pondered whether a paradisal
state could be reconciled with our "gradual evolutionary origins,"
even going so far as to say that, "The cosmos would bring pain
and death to man even if they were not continually rising from
within himself."[18] What we do know is that God offered the first

humans the invitation to loving communion with him and the sanctifying grace to respond in obedience. At any rate, such a short span of time would quickly perish from human memory, especially considering that human life became inundated by sinful tendencies, separation from God, suffering, and death.

St. Thomas notes that we are not entirely deprived of reason, goodwill, strength, and so on, but that we are deeply wounded in these capacities. He calls this loss of preternatural gifts a "wounding of *nature*." When we define human nature only by our physical and biological heritage, then it makes no sense to call the loss of gifts that go beyond that heritage a "wounding." If man is defined simply as a particular primate species, then what Thomas calls wounds are not wounds at all; the good and bad to which our instincts incline us are, from the biological perspective, simply an expression of our nature.

St. Thomas, however, was not thinking of human nature only as a matter of our biological heritage. He was thinking of human nature in regard to what God ultimately intends us to be: what the second-century bishop St. Irenaeus of Lyons meant when he said that man is properly composed not only of body and soul, but also "receiving the the Holy Spirit."[19] Just as this kind of body cries to God out of justice for a rational soul, so a living man or woman, body and soul, cries out for the ability to embody all the goodness that he or she is capable of. Thanks to understanding and freedom, we are capable of so much more than what our biological heritage offers us.

St. Thomas confirms this when he asserts that, after the Fall, the first humans simply reverted to their biological heritage, to the state of a rational animal without grace: "When man turned his back on God, he fell under the influence of his sensual [bodily] impulses . . . [after the Fall] he is likened to beasts that are led by the impulse of sensuality . . . a deviation from the law of reason."[20] Here St. Thomas, who knows nothing of evolution, genetics, paleoanthropology, or evolutionary psychology, sees that what we are by nature is "the rational and the irrational constant-ly jostling."[21] Reflecting upon this quote from St. Thomas, the theologian Henri Rondet helps us see how the evil tendencies we find in ourselves are both natural from the scientific perspective and yet unnatural from the divine perspective: "Man has been left to his nature; but it is precisely this that is the paradox and stumbling block. Death, suffering, ignorance, the revolt of the senses—all this is in fact natural, since man is made of flesh and spirit. *But what is natural to an animal organism becomes unnatural for a soul made in the image of God.*"[22]

In light of this, the wound caused by original sin, our fallen state, is best understood as a supernatural spark that was snuffed out by sin, a higher way of life that was lost—because of sin, the human person was left unfinished. God had more gifts to give, but he did not get to bestow them—he was stopped. Like the wise and loving father in the Parable of the Prodigal Son (see Luke 15:11–32), he respected the freedom of his children and permitted them to go away. As the *Catechism* explains:

> Man, tempted by the devil, let his trust in his Creator die in his heart and, abusing his freedom, disobeyed God's command. This is what man's first sin consisted of. All subsequent sin would be disobedience toward God and lack of trust in his goodness. In that sin man *preferred* himself to God and by that very act scorned him. He chose himself over and against God, against

the requirements of his creaturely status and therefore
against his own good.[23]

With original sin, death—the natural end of all biological
life—made its entrance into *human* history.[24] Worst of all, our
friendship with God was broken. As a consequence, human history became "inundated by sin."[25] The state of separation from
God caused by the Fall, in the words of the *Catechism*, "is a
sin 'contracted' and 'not committed'"—a state and not an act.
Human nature has been wounded by original sin, but not totally
corrupted; the image of God has been disfigured and stained but
still remains.[26]

With original sin we once again come upon a doctrine that
is easily misunderstood. Some have speculated that the transmis-
sion of original sin to all human beings involves some biological
defect, as if the human genome was altered by the moral evil
committed by our first parents. Original sin is not something that
is passed on like an infectious disease or a birth defect. St. Thomas
Aquinas rejects this idea, although he affirms that original sin is
passed on by sexual generation, "transmitted with human nature,"
in the words of St. Paul VI (1897–1978).[27] Aquinas asserts that
we should think of all human beings as if they were one man,
"Adam," like the members of a single bodily organism.[28]

Pope Benedict XVI approached the mystery of original sin
from the perspective of human personhood and relationships.
Being "in the image of God" means that we are persons who
are capable of communion, bonding with other persons in close
relationships. Our lives make no sense without being in loving
relationships with each other. Sin is the disturbance of relationships; whenever I sin, I make myself the center of the universe,
rejecting God and others. Therefore, the first sin damaged the

network of relationships at the very beginning of human history. The world of human community we all enter at the beginning of our existence "is marked by relational damage":

> At the very moment that a person enters human existence, which is a good, he or she is confronted by a sin-damaged world. Each of us enters into a situation in which relationality has been hurt. Consequently each person is, from the very start, damaged in relationships and does not engage in them as he or she ought. Sin pursues the human being, and he or she capitulates to it.[29]

Decades later, Benedict would complete this insight with a beautiful contrast: the nature of human sinfulness as slavery versus the sinless freedom of the Blessed Virgin Mary, who was preserved from all stain of sin from the moment of her conception. We all carry the "drop of poison" of thinking that by standing all alone, raising ourselves to God's level, we will fulfill ourselves and find real happiness. "We call this drop of poison 'original sin,'" Benedict explained. In sinning, every human being "sets his sights on power, with which he desires to take his own life autonomously in hand. And in doing so, he trusts in deceit rather than in truth and thereby sinks with his life into emptiness, into death."[30]

But God's love and the love of others are gifts; trying to sinfully stand on our own is to enslave ourselves, for the freedom we have must be lived "with one another, and for one another," in order for it to be realized. Mary, on the other hand, shows us what freedom really means:

> The person who abandons himself totally in God's hands does not become God's puppet, a boring "yes man"; he does not lose his freedom. Only the person who entrusts himself totally to God finds true freedom, the great, creative immensity of the freedom of good.
>
> The person who turns to God does not become smaller but greater, for through God and with God he becomes great, he becomes divine, he becomes truly himself. The person who puts himself in God's hands does not distance himself from others, withdrawing into his private salvation; on the contrary, it is only then that his heart truly awakens and he becomes a sensitive, hence, benevolent and open person.
>
> The closer a person is to God, the closer he is to people. We see this in Mary. The fact that she is totally with God is the reason why she is so close to human beings.[31]

Mary is our sign of hope that the cycle of sin can be broken and our humanity made complete. She is the object of our hope only as one who points to her son, who is the perfect answer to the dilemma of our sinfulness and the tendencies toward it we have by nature. In his life, death, and resurrection, Jesus moved the dividing line between good and evil out of the human heart, leaving only the good.

We will focus on this shortly, but first we must briefly return to a question we addressed in the last chapter: How many "first parents" sinned? It does not seem to be a wild leap, in light of the most recent discoveries, to consider Adam and Eve as symbolic of a community, the first community to make the breakthrough to rationality and freedom. Perhaps the first of our kind to make the breakthrough from potential to actual symbolic thought, language, and reason also turned quickly away from the goodness being offered by God, and then drew the others in their community into a way of being human marked by "relational damage," into a community characterized by sin.

Of course this is speculation, but speculation is essential to all human thought. Much like scientists, theologians often find themselves having to go back to the data and challenge their assumptions. This is not a threat to faith, in which we entrust ourselves to God despite the limits of our understanding. In fact, it refines and purifies faith to find itself faced with new questions, and it is through such faithful theological reflection that our understanding of divine truth moves forward.[32] The Blessed Virgin Mary, who asked the angel Gabriel, "How can this be, since I have no relations with a man?" regarding his announcement that she would "conceive . . . and bear a son" (Lk 1:34, 31) is the model for all theological speculation. Questions are not bad; faith is not blind.

It is, furthermore, worth noting that what is being reconsidered here is not the question of *whether* an original sin occurred and fundamentally altered the manner in which all human beings henceforth live and experience their humanity, finding themselves in need of a divine Savior and Redeemer. Rather, what is being reconsidered here in light of the progress of modern science is how we ought to interpret *the context in which* this original sin took place. The substance of the faith itself is not what is at issue, only our understanding of how we ought best to comprehend and articulate it in a reasonable and responsible manner. As Ratzinger said in his 1964 lectures, "That mankind's first decision was characterized by a 'no' is essential. Whether this beginning was determined by one or more is not so important."[33]

In the end, however, sin did enter the world, and no matter how many first parents were involved, there can be no doubt that it affected humanity in a universal way. But much more important than how many humans were involved is how its destructive power is overcome. As noted above, Jesus Christ has pushed the line dividing good and evil out of the human heart. And it is to his Sacred Heart that we now turn.

THE SACRED HEART OF JESUS

In its Constitution on the Church in the Modern World, the Second Vatican Council identified Christ as the "Final Adam," the one who "fully reveals man to himself and makes his supreme calling clear." Continuing this line of thought, the Council points to Christ as the perfect human being:

> He Who is "the image of the invisible God" (Col. 1:15), is Himself the perfect man. To the sons of Adam He restores the divine likeness which had been disfigured from the first sin onward. . . . For by His incarnation the Son of God has united Himself in some fashion with *every human being*. He worked with human hands, He thought with a human mind, acted by human choice and *loved with a human heart*. Born of the Virgin Mary, He has truly been made one of us, like us in all things except sin.[34]

In this short summary of the mystery of the Incarnation, we see the solution to the dark riddle of human existence when it is only considered from the biological and philosophical perspectives. Christ answers the ambiguity of our moral fragility and inclinations toward evil with perfect love, living out an ordinary human existence in an extraordinary way. He did not take up human nature as it existed before sin damaged human life, endowed with preternatural gifts. His human nature was not fallen, but the nature he assumed had all of the effects of a fallen nature in order to redeem it, purifying it through the abundance of his love and his perfect obedience to the will of the Father.

The key phrase in this important text from Vatican II is its assertion that Jesus "loved with a human heart." In biblical symbolism, the heart represents the center of thinking, willing, and acting. With this in mind, the Church annually celebrates the Feast of the Sacred Heart of Jesus as a reminder of the pure love with which Jesus loved all human beings and united himself to us totally and irrevocably. In chapter 1 we recognized that the love by which God creates the universe is a love springing from mercy, which causes goodness where goodness is absent. In the revelation of Jesus Christ, the Word made flesh, even the "holes in being" created by sin and moral evil are met with a mercy and a loving power that draws good out of evil.

The author of the Letter to the Hebrews captures this beautifully. Christ, he tells us, has become our "merciful and faithful high priest" precisely by loving us in the midst of his own human suffering and temptations: "Because he himself was tested through what he suffered, he is able to help those who are being tested" (2:18). Recognizing that Jesus faced the same struggles that we face, the author also tells us that this was necessary for our sake: "For we do not have a high priest who is unable to sympathize with our weaknesses, but one who has similarly been tested in every way, yet without sin. So let us confidently approach the throne of grace to receive mercy and to find grace for timely help" (4:15–16). Jesus reversed the disobedience of sin by persevering through his suffering and temptations in obedience to his Father and so became "the source of eternal salvation for all who obey him" (5:9).

The process of salvation, by which we slowly start to regather the riches lost through sin, begins when we enter into the mystical Body of Christ, the Church, through the sacrament of Baptism. In Baptism, the tragic alienation of "the sin of Adam" is replaced by a redemptive unity in Christ, the Final Adam, who has broken the chains of sin and death. As the *Catechism* states, "Baptism not only purifies from all sins, but also makes the [baptized] 'a new creature,' an adopted son of God, who has become a 'partaker of the divine nature,' member of Christ and co-heir with him, and a temple of the Holy Spirit."[35] The reception of this sacrament does not annihilate or replace our biological human nature; we remain fundamentally the same human being after Baptism as before. And yet, through this and the other sacraments, as well as through a life of prayer, through communion with fellow Christians, through sacrifice, through care for others, and through the practice of virtue, the translation of our humanity into this new way of life in Christ not only is possible, but also has the guarantee of a divine promise. As we pray in the Preface of the Mass that opens the Eucharistic Prayer, "In love You created us, in justice You condemned us, but in mercy You redeemed us, through Jesus Christ our Lord."

SLAVE OF THE SLAVES

The love and holiness described above is not something seen only in Christ and the Blessed Virgin Mary. It is a theme that runs throughout the lives of all holy men and women, the great

Communion of Saints whom the Church holds up for us as examples and as our powerful intercessors. We began this chapter by honestly facing the human inclination toward outgroup bias which, when unchecked, turns into nightmarish forms of violence against "outsiders." Let us now look at how the opposite can happen when the light shining from the Sacred Heart of Jesus shines upon ours.

One of the most horrific embodiments of violence in human history is racial slavery; the capture, bondage, and forced labor of Africans is a dark phase in the history of the colonization of the Americas. For two and a half centuries, until 1852, the slave trade was active, and it is estimated that about 125,000 Africans entered the port city of Cartagena, Colombia, in chains between 1595 and 1640. Each ship would carry four hundred to five hundred slaves, and it was not uncommon for a third of those to die on the two-month voyage. It would have been a hopeless situation were it not for heroic Christians like St. Peter Claver.

Claver was born to a wealthy family in Catalonia, Spain. During his university studies he encountered the Society of Jesus (the Jesuits) and joined them, and shortly thereafter he met a Jesuit brother who helped him realize a call from the Lord to go to the New World. In 1611, he arrived in Cartagena and was ordained a priest in 1616. There he became an assistant to Fr. Alonso de Sandoval, who first began the outreach to African slaves. Then he began his own work, becoming a "slave to the slaves." Over the span of thirty-five years, he never missed the arrival of a ship. He would board the ships, bathe the slaves in perfumed water, and give them clean water to drink. He would carry gifts of food and would care for the sick. Over the years he would travel widely to visit those whom he had once cared for on the ships and continued his ministry to them. By his witness of faith and his selfless acts of love, more than three hundred thousand slaves would be baptized by his hands.

The lengths to which St. Peter Claver went to care for these slaves showed a depth of love that was truly supernatural, far surpassing any kind of natural empathy or compassion:

> Claver would wipe the sweat from the faces of the slaves with his own handkerchief. Moreover, he would often clothe the sick and diseased in his own cloak. As some of his interpreters witnessed, the cloak had to be washed up to seven times a day from the stink and filth which it had accumulated. It was routine for Claver to console his fellow man by joyfully undertaking practices which were considered extremely repugnant to most. As one eye-witness notes, "Most admirable was that he not only cleansed these plague-ridden ulcers with the two handkerchiefs he kept for that, but did not hesitate to press his lips to them." He plainly saw Christ "in the least of these brethren."[36]

It may be a natural inclination for human beings to fear and distrust those who are different. Yet when that inclination is hardened into evil choices and habits, whole cultures are corrupted. What we see in St. Peter Claver is the "new natural"—the recognition that all human beings are brothers and sisters, a realization made possible by the grace of God given to us in Christ. As the words of St. Paul reveal, this "new natural" involves replacing bias with belonging: "There is neither Jew nor Greek, there is neither slave nor free person, there is not male or female; for you are all one in Christ Jesus" (Gal 3:28).

This perspective is not unique to St. Peter Claver and St. Paul; it is at the heart of the new reality of human life that radiates from the Sacred Heart of Jesus Christ. From the beginning of Christianity, we see a new standard dawning in the world: the conviction that ethnicity, culture, and color do not make anyone inferior or worthy of maltreatment, slavery, or death, and that love must extend beyond the boundaries created by "family and tribe." In the words of sociologist Rodney Stark in his study of the rise of Christianity from its origins as a tiny movement in Palestine to becoming the majority religion of the Roman Empire, "What Christianity gave to its converts was nothing less than their humanity. In this sense virtue *was* its own reward."[37]

The work of God in fashioning his image, postponed by sin, has been definitively accomplished by Christ, who invites all human beings to freely join him in this new way of being human. As we will see in the next chapter, this fantastic mystery has remade the universe and the human race. In fact, it has revealed where the true origin of humanity is to be discovered: neither in the relics of prehistory that we find in Blombos, nor in the advent of language and symbolism, but in the manger that we find in Bethlehem and in the man who showed us what it means to be truly human: Jesus, the "Final Adam."

6.

FROM EVOLUTION TO RESURRECTION: JESUS, THE FINAL ADAM

> In reality it is only in the mystery of the Word made flesh that the mystery of man truly becomes clear. For Adam, the first man, was a type of him who was to come, Christ the Lord. Christ the new Adam, in the very revelation of the mystery of the Father and of his love, fully reveals man to himself and brings to light his most high calling.
>
> —Vatican II, *Gaudium et Spes*

AN IMAGE IN STONE

The Cathedral of Chartres in France is the most beautiful building I have ever seen, the greatest architectural accomplishment of the Catholic culture of the Middle Ages. It was built to be a complete account of the history of salvation, and it includes creation as one of its artistic themes. One example is found on the exterior, among the exquisitely carved images on the north porch of the cathedral. There we find an image depicting the formation of Adam, based on a verse from Genesis with which we are already familiar: "Then the LORD God formed the man out of the dust of the ground and blew into his nostrils the breath of life, and the man became a living being" (2:7). The medieval master of stone might have appreciated the beautiful paradox that he was sculpting God as a sculptor and crafting an image of God forming his own image. Regardless, he had a surprise in mind, at least a surprise for modern eyes, as he chipped and chiseled.

In this sculpture a sleeping human being clings to the divine sculptor's knee, his head reclined almost on his lap. His lower body is only partially formed out of the clay lump that rests to the lower right side of the image. The divine sculptor is moving his hands gently and skillfully under and above the man's head, each hand actively sculpting him. But when we look at the face of the divine sculptor, with its careful attention to his masterpiece, we find a surprise; the face is not that of an elderly man by which medieval art often represented God the Father, "the Ancient of Days" (Dn 7:9). The face is the face of Christ—he is the divine sculptor who is forming Adam.

In chapter 1 we observed that the divine Son is the one through whom God creates the universe, the *Logos* who gives to all things their orderliness and intelligibility. This sculpture adds another dimension to the consideration of human life: we are the image of God not simply by nature, by which we are an imperfect image of God, but by being formed by Christ, the *Logos*-made-flesh, into the image of his perfect humanity. In the words of the International Theological Commission:

> The origins of man are to be found in Christ: for he
> is created "through him and in him" (Col 1:16), "the
> Word [who is] the life . . . and the light of every man
> who is coming into the world" (Jn 1:3–4, 9). While it is

> true that man is created *ex nihilo*, it can also be said that
> he is created from the fullness of Christ himself who is
> at once the creator, the mediator and the end of man.[1]

In other words the first "Adam," symbolic of the first human beings, was simply a preparation for the real goal of the creation of humanity: the Final Adam, who fulfills what began long ago. Here's the lesson the sculpture offers us—if we define ourselves only by the first Adam, we fail to discover and realize the fullness of our humanity as intended and willed by God.

BACK TO THE BEGINNING

To see how sacred scripture and sacred Tradition together testify to this truth, we have to return to the First Creation Account. If you are familiar with that opening passage of the entire Bible, you probably have noticed the very rhythmic, almost formulaic way in which each day of creation is depicted as unfolding. First, God speaks. Second, what he speaks happens—this is indicated either by the statement of the fact ("and there was light") or with "and so it happened." Third, he sees that what he has made is good—he beholds that goodness, and that goodness is declared: "God saw that it was good." Finally, an end to the day is announced: "Evening came, and morning followed—the sixth day" are the last words of Genesis 1; the seventh day is depicted as the first verses of Genesis 2.

Now on the sixth day, God creates twice. First he makes the land animals, then he makes human beings. When God makes the land animals, the narrative follows the expected pattern; but when he makes us, the pattern is broken.

There is no "Let there be"; instead, there is an act of planning, "Let us make," as if a long process is about to occur. And there is no immediate "and so it happened" after God makes human beings; that only comes after God gives human beings his commands for them to "be fertile and multiply" and so on. But the most unsettling omission is that God never directly declares the goodness of humanity. Of course there is no doubt that humans are the summit of God's creation, and they are certainly good according to their being creatures of God, who only produces good things. In fact, only when human beings are in the world does God behold everything he has made and declare it "very good." But human moral goodness is never declared at the end of the sixth day, nor does God "behold" (in Hebrew, *yar*) what he has made when he makes human beings. This could indicate that the Lord is not finished with the formation of his image; he is awaiting the human response.

In summary, God's "human project" is incomplete at the end of Genesis 1. In fact, even the words "and so it happened," which follow the other acts of creation, are mysteriously absent.[2] Equally curious is the omission of any declaration of an end to the seventh day, the final day of creation, God's Sabbath rest, in Genesis 2:3—no "evening came, and morning followed." "Curiouser and curiouser," as Alice would say in Lewis Carroll's *Alice in Wonderland*, or as we would say, "What is up with *that*!"

Now these omissions may have had some original meaning that we don't know about, and scholars argue for various hypotheses as to why the text was written with these omissions. Some think they might not have had any original significance. For historians and biblical scholars, this is a perfectly valid line of inquiry. But regardless of what might have originally been intended, Catholic theology sees all scripture as pointing forward to Christ in some way. These omissions are like the blanks in a math problem that await being resolved; they demand a new solution. And when we come to the New Testament, we see the finished equation, for as St. Irenaeus would say in the late second century, Jesus "brought all the newness, by bringing himself."[3]

JESUS IS THE ANSWER

When we get to the gospels, we find that the pattern of the First Creation Account was not broken, just not completed. Let's start with God's first words as he begins to make humans; these words are not a present act of making but a kind of future planning: "Let us make" (Gn 1:26), unlike the more definite "Let there be" on the previous days of creation (cf. Gn 1:3). When we arrive at the Annunciation of the angel Gabriel to Mary in Luke's gospel (1:26–38), Mary responds to the angel Gabriel's message that she will be the mother of Jesus by saying something similar to God's previous words of creation, "Let it be": "Let it be to me according to your word." The Lord of heaven and earth lifts Mary up into the creative act by allowing his creative word to be uttered by her! The angel has just promised her that "the holy Spirit will come upon" her. Compare that to Genesis 1:2, which says "a mighty wind [was] sweeping over the waters"—the Hebrew words for "wind" and "spirit" are the same. Just as the Holy Spirit was present at creation, so also the Holy Spirit is present at the Annunciation, as in Mary's womb will be the genesis of a new creation—a new origin for humanity.

We also find in the gospels the missing "it was good" in regard to human beings. The undeclared goodness of humanity is finally proclaimed near the beginning of the Gospel of Matthew, when Jesus submits himself to the baptism of John the Baptist in order "to fulfill all righteousness" (3:15). As soon as he receives baptism, the voice of God is heard: "After Jesus was baptized, he came up from the water and behold, the heavens were opened [for him], and he saw the Spirit of God descending like a dove [and] coming upon him. And a voice came from the heavens, saying, 'This is my beloved Son, with whom I am well pleased'" (Mt 3:16–17). In the Jewish "equation" of God's will, righteousness = goodness = God's good pleasure. In other words, as Jesus humbly submits himself publicly to the Father's will, lining up with sinners even though he is sinless, God's declaration of pleasure indicates that in Jesus the goodness he intended for humanity has been finally and fully achieved—a human being has arrived who pleases God in every way and who is perfectly good. The disobedience with which human history began, which postponed the completion of humanity, has now been overcome.

Another omission in the First Creation Account is closely connected to this one. In Genesis the formula is not just "it was good," but "God saw that it was good" (cf. Gn 1:10)—a beholding of goodness. With this in mind let's turn to the narrative of Christ's passion in John's gospel:

> Then Pilate took Jesus and had him scourged. And the soldiers wove a crown out of thorns and placed it on his head, and clothed him in a purple cloak, and they came to him and said, "Hail, King of the Jews!" And they struck him repeatedly. Once more Pilate went out and said to them, "Look, I am bringing him out to you, so that you may know that I find no guilt in him." So Jesus came out, wearing the crown of thorns and the

> purple cloak. And he said to them, "Behold, the man!" When the chief priests and the guards saw him they cried out, "Crucify him, crucify him!" Pilate said to them, "Take him yourselves and crucify him. I find no guilt in him." (Jn 19:1–6)

In the Gospel of John we finally discover the divine "behold" in reference to human beings. After Pontius Pilate has Jesus scourged, he has him brought before the crowd and declares, "*Idou ho anthrōpos*!" in English "Behold the human being!" The missing "behold" which we expect to come in Genesis at the creation of human beings appears where we least expect it, on the lips of Jesus' cynical, unbelieving judge. In God's providential plan, these words are as much the words of God the Father as they are the words of the Roman governor. Through Jesus' unjust judge God gives us the "behold," signaling that in Christ's loving sacrifice, in his obedience to his Father, and in his love for us, we finally see what God intended for us to be. Only in Jesus' loving sacrifice is the making of humanity completed. In the words of theologian John Behr, "Christ, over whom death had no claim so that he genuinely went voluntarily to his death, conquering death by his death, is the first true human being in history. He *is* the image of the invisible God (Col 1:15)."[4]

As Jesus breathes his dying breath, he says, "It is finished," and John tells us, "And bowing his head, he handed over the spirit" (Jn 19:30). Jesus' words offer the missing "end" to the seventh "day" of the First Creation Account. With the completion of his sacrifice, God's greatest project, the human person, is also complete. Christ "hands over the spirit," the Gift-Love of God, to the rest of humanity, so that we can find the completion of our own humanity in union with him. Although John doesn't mention it, in all three synoptic gospels darkness sweeps over the land due to an eclipse of the sun. And so, as Christ hangs on the Cross, "evening came, and morning followed"—the seventh day has finally ended, and the new day of the Resurrection is dawning.

THE FINAL ADAM

At the heart of the New Testament message, when read as a fulfillment of the First Creation Account, is the recognition that Jesus Christ is the true human being in every respect, the new and Final Adam, the master of a new creation. While St. Matthew and St. John present this to us symbolically, St. Paul is more direct:

> So, too, it is written, "The first man, Adam, became a living being," the last Adam a life-giving spirit. But the spiritual was not first; rather the natural and then the spiritual. The first man was from the earth, earthly; the second man, from heaven. As was the earthly one, so also are the earthly, and as is the heavenly one, so also are the heavenly. Just as we have borne the image of the earthly one, we shall also bear the image of the heavenly one. (1 Cor 15:45–49)

Here St. Paul extends the concept of humanity beyond that which we are given in Genesis.

In his Letter to the Romans, St. Paul tells us that the first Adam is a *type* of Christ: "Adam, who is the type of the one who was to come" (5:14). In theology, a type is something or someone that prefigures a new and greater reality, called its *antitype* by theologians. For example, the Crossing of the Red Sea (type) points to Christian baptism (antitype), in which humans are freed from the slavery of sin, a much greater liberation than the deliverance of the Israelites from slavery in Egypt. In a type-antitype relationship, also known as a *typological relationship*, the antitype is everything that the type was, but in a new and greater way. Jesus the human being is everything Adam was, everything we are, but in a way that fulfills what we were meant to be. As noted in chapter 5, it is not in the mists of prehistory, in Blombos Cave, or in some as-yet-undiscovered place, but only in the manger in Bethlehem—and even more so on Calvary—that humanity really has its origin. The creation of humans began far in the past, but it only reached its completion and its true "beginning" in Christ thousands of years later. He gives humanity a new origin, its true origin, in the plan of God.

What is it about Christ that makes him the Final Adam, the true human being? According to Pope Benedict XVI, it is his radical dependence upon God and his openness to us. Jesus knows that being fully human as God intended means being entirely for God and for others. He knows that the human creature only realizes her fullest potential by moving beyond herself, by finding herself insufficient when she is by herself and only for herself. As Jesus tells us in Luke 9:24: "For whoever wishes to save his life will lose it, but whoever loses his life for my sake will save it." Only through being with and for others does *Homo sapiens* come to be fully human—and the "other" above all is God. In Christ the image of God becomes pure openness to God, which is what man was made to be.

The fact that Jesus Christ is the Final Adam, the true man, means that his existence concerns all who are called *ādām*— that is, all human beings. The sculpture at Chartres Cathedral is showing us not something that happened way back then, but a real possibility, indeed a promise, for *now*. Jesus is not some unrealizable ideal that stands above us, showing us how incomplete and broken we are so that we can despair of ever achieving true fulfillment and everlasting happiness. To call him the Final Adam is to say that it is in him that all humanity is to be gathered into completion.

This is the meaning of the opening of his body on the Cross, the climax of the whole Passion narrative in John's gospel: "But when they came to Jesus and saw that he was already dead, they did not break his legs, but one soldier thrust his lance into his side, and immediately blood and water flowed out" (Jn 19:33–34). The opening of Jesus' side is symbolic of his interior openness to include us within his life. Now, from his pierced side, a new humanity can be formed, as prefigured in the symbolic image of the creation of Eve from the side of the sleeping Adam in the Second Creation Account (see Genesis 2:20–25). Jesus lets the walls of his existence be broken down; rather than this ending his existence, his unbounded life flows out and carries all human beings who believe in him back into it. The redeemed human beings, who are saved by the blood and water that flow out of the Final Adam, we call the Body of Christ, the Church.

BECOMING FULLY HUMAN

It is not surprising, then, to discover that the earliest Christians considered their union with Christ, and their imitation of him, to be an essential part of the process of becoming human. In the first decade of the second century of the Christian era, around AD 110, a bishop from the Holy Land, St. Ignatius of Antioch, made his way to Rome under escort of Roman soldiers as a prisoner on his way to martyrdom. Along the way he wrote letters to the various Christian communities in the places along his route: Smyrna, Philadelphia, Ephesus, and others. He also wrote ahead to the Church in Rome, and he made an urgent appeal to the Christians there not to attempt to avert his execution. He closes with the request that they allow him to undergo martyrdom:

> The time for my birth is close at hand. Forgive me, my brothers. Do not stand in the way of my birth to real life; do not wish me stillborn. My desire is to belong to God. . . . *Only on my arrival there can I be fully a human being.*[5]

Full humanity, therefore, comes from living and loving as Christ did. The human being who shows us the real meaning of life and the path to unending happiness is not the one at the beginning of the Bible but the one who appears at the end.

It is easy to misunderstand this important Christian truth, especially because it comes in the context of Jesus' painful death. What makes Christ the fulfillment of our humanity, the Final Adam, is not the grisliness of his death but the perfection of his love. This love is what makes his sacrifice for us perfect and complete. As St. Augustine once observed, a true sacrifice is an "act done for the purpose of clinging to God in a holy fellowship . . . directed to that final Good which makes possible our true happiness."[6] St. Ignatius of Antioch saw in his own martyrdom a chance to perfect both his love and his humanity. But it is in the Christian life, which always involves clinging to God and loving one's neighbor, that the process of becoming "fully a human being" is possible for all of us. The Christian life is the adventure in which the image of God is completed in all who believe by being refashioned into the very image of Christ.

To become fully human, to repent of sin and believe in the Gospel, the Good News of Jesus Christ, means finally to open ourselves to the man who was fully God. Ultimately, every human being draws near to him whenever they forget themselves and love selflessly and in truth, and the Church teaches us to hope that there are and have been non-Christians who have come very close to him without even knowing him explicitly, as "[God] wills everyone to be saved and to come to knowledge of the truth" (1 Tm 2:4).[7] The Christian life is the explicit awareness and full acceptance of the real meaning of being human: to be like Christ, which is to be fully and entirely with and for others. Christian formation, which is also called discipleship, is not simply a lifestyle choice. As Pope Benedict XVI once wrote, being Christian is also not "the result of an ethical choice or a lofty idea."[8] From the divine perspective, Christian discipleship is nothing less than an encounter with the person and event of Jesus Christ and the completion of what hominin evolution began. It is a completion that leads to a life that never ends.

THE GREATEST "LEAP"

In our last lesson we recognized the self-offering of Jesus as our salvation, the completion of our humanity. But Jesus did not only die; we believe that he rose to an entirely new and indestructible kind of life, a life beyond the biological kind that we have by nature and that he had by virtue of the Incarnation—a life sustained by oxygen, nutrients, and so on. His resurrection was a real historical event that shattered the dimensions of history and transcended it. The Resurrection brings us to a new horizon in which matter, space, and time are enveloped by divine love and power.

Without the Resurrection of Jesus, Christianity is absurd and its promises are false. St. Paul openly declared this when he said, "If Christ has not been raised, then empty [too] is our preaching; empty, too, your faith" (1 Cor 15:14). If Jesus is merely dead, then death, the natural biological end of all life, is all that awaits each of us. The problem of physical and moral evil overshadows any hope we might have for everlasting happiness. What God has revealed in the Resurrection of Christ is that his eternal decision to create the world is simply one glimmer of the immense love he has for humanity. So, it is all-important that we understand what the word *resurrection* means. Pope Benedict XVI taught:

> Jesus's Resurrection was about breaking out into an entirely new form of life, into a life that is no longer subject to the law of dying and becoming, but lies beyond it—a life that opens up a new dimension of human existence. Therefore the Resurrection of Jesus is not an isolated event, that we could set aside as something limited to the past, but it constitutes an "evolutionary leap" . . . in Jesus's Resurrection a new possibility of human existence is obtained that affects everyone and that opens up a future, a new kind of future, for mankind.[9]

Resurrection, therefore, is something that concerns not only Jesus but, rather, all of us. It is not simply a resuscitated corpse's return to a normal human life. Instead, it is a "leap" to a whole new kind of life, which Jesus makes first but that is also promised to all humanity. This is what is meant when in the Creed we profess to believe in the "resurrection of the body and life everlasting."

THE RESURRECTION AND SCIENCE

Considering the Resurrection with modern science as a backdrop helps us look upon it with fresh eyes. From the perspective of physics, the Resurrection is the elevation of matter to a new way of existing beyond what is possible in the normal state of the universe. From the perspective of biology, the man Jesus, body and soul, now belongs totally to the sphere of the divine and eternal. Now, "in" God there is a place for bodiliness, which means that human beings now have a "place" in God's life. This also means that our entire universe is subject to renewal and redemption. As St. Augustine recognized long ago, we come from the very texture of the elements; the universe is within us as much as we are within it. And so, in the resurrection of the body, the whole cosmos will be affected; "the whole creation will become song."[10]

Does our faith in the Resurrection of Jesus contradict reason and a proper respect for the integrity of nature? This would be the case only if we turned bodily resurrection into a function of nature, or if we saw it as the violation of nature by divine power. But the miracle of the Resurrection would be a "violation" of nature only if nature is something that doesn't first already exist within the eternal "let there be" of God, who is nature's true Creator and Source of Being to all things. The Resurrection is about the ultimate destiny of nature, the "new heavens and a new earth" (2 Pt 3:13), which God intends. If science is polluted by an unjustified commitment to reductionism—the idea that all real things are *only* the sum of their parts—then not only will resurrection and life after death seem absurd, but so will life *before* death, because for the reductionist the living things we see are only collections of parts, acting as the sum of those parts.[11]

The resurrection of the dead is intelligible only if we see it in the context of God's plan for the universe. Thanks to God's loving providence, and not simply by its own power, the universe is journeying to a fulfillment in which physical and moral evil will be no more. If this is the case, then the Resurrection and, indeed, all authentic miracles are streams of light breaking through the ordinary, temporary, imperfect "old order" (Rv 21:4) of things. The Resurrection is the advent of a new set of laws for the universe through which the material universe will perfectly radiate the higher, spiritual realities of love and freedom.

One person who saw miracles in this way was the great southern Catholic novelist Flannery O'Connor (1925–1964). In response to a friend for whom miracles were an obstacle to accepting the Christian faith because they seemed to violate natural laws, O'Connor took the reverse perspective:

> For my part I think that when I know what the laws of the flesh and the physical really are, then I will know what God is. We know them as we see them, not as God sees them. For me it is the virgin birth, the Incarnation, the resurrection which are the true laws of the flesh and the physical. Death, decay, destruction are the suspension of these laws. . . . The resurrection of Christ seems [to me] the high point of the law of nature.[12]

In a similar fashion, the Catholic convert and poet Richard Crashaw (1612–1649) interpreted the Miracle of Cana, when Jesus turned water into wine, precisely as the water "blushing" in the presence of its Lord and Maker![13] When the new order of things begins to break through, we discover *all* that nature can do when God is fully present to it and when it is conformed to

God's will for it. God reaches "downward" to creation so that nature can reach "upward" to God.

Benedict XVI asked the question: "Does the Resurrection contradict science?" In his answer he combines a thorough respect for faith, reason, and the integrity of nature, while also bidding us to be open to the possibility of something beyond our experience: "Naturally, there can be no contradiction of clear scientific data. The Resurrection accounts certainly speak of something outside the world of our experience. They speak of something new, something unprecedented—a new dimension of reality that is revealed. What already exists is not called into question. Rather we are told that there is a further dimension, beyond what was previously known."[14] With this in mind, the Resurrection does not require that we deny what we see in history and the universe, but that we see them against the backdrop of God's love. As we learned in chapter 1 from Julian of Norwich, all things have existence from the love of God; he is to all things the Source of Being. And so, the Source of the universe and all its creatures has the power to beckon us beyond the limits of biological life.

THE LAST SHALL BE FIRST: FROM BIOS TO ZOĒ

The key to understanding the Resurrection is the reality of love. In the Resurrection, the final stage of human evolution reverses the paradigm of existence. In the first phase of human existence, biological life is necessary in order to love. In his sacrificial death, Jesus valued love more highly than the biological life that made it possible. His resurrection tells us that, although in this existence one must first have biological life in order to love, the power of love is greater than the power of the merely biological. In the Resurrection, biology is encompassed by and incorporated into the power of love. And so love makes it possible for us to transcend the limits of biological existence.

After his resurrection, Christ did not go back to his previous earthly life, as did Lazarus whom he had raised from the dead (see John 11:1–44). He rose to a definitive new life no longer governed by the chemical and biological laws that govern our lives now. In this new reality love is the foundation of life, and, therefore, in love life becomes indestructible. He who loved us to the end has founded our immortality on that love. This is why scripture says that Christ is our life: "When Christ your life appears, then you too will appear with him in glory" (Col 3:4). If he has risen, then we will too, for in his risen humanity he loves us now and always. If he is not risen, then we will not rise either, for then the situation is that death still has the last word, nothing else. Our own love, left to itself, cannot overcome death; taken in itself, our own love would have to remain a feeble unanswered cry for resurrection and eternal life. But when Christ's love envelops our love, then our own immortality has a foundation that can be neither shaken nor removed.

Thus, a new kind of life has dawned in the world through the Final Adam. In the Resurrection of Christ the realm of biological evolution has been left behind. In Christ humanity has "leapt" to a quite different plane, in which love is no longer subject to biology but supports it. As Jesus himself once said to his disciples, the last has become the first (see Matthew 20:16). The final stage of "evolution" (actually, the leap beyond it!) is no longer a biological stage; the dominion of biology has ended. And since biology, or *bios*, always involves death, the sovereignty of death has ended as well. Christ has opened up the realm that the Bible calls, in the original Greek, *zoē*—that is, definitive life not qualified or restricted by biology, life that has left behind the rule of death. The last stage of evolution needed by the world to reach its goal has been achieved within the realm of biology by Jesus, who through his death and resurrection brings humanity past the purely biological realm.

Of course, our faith tells us that the mode of our personal participation in immortality will depend upon our mode of living. If we place life above love, or self-interest above others, then we begin hell right now on earth. The Resurrection of Christ reveals the tragic dimension of sin even more deeply. The definition of sin is for one to be "caved in on oneself"—the exact opposite of Christ's openness to God and neighbor. Bishop Robert Barron shows us the absurdity of sin: "The powers of the human soul, which are meant to orient us to nature and other human beings and the cosmos and finally the infinite mystery of God, are focused on the tiny and infinitely uninteresting ego [self]. Like a black hole, the sinful soul draws all the light and energy around it into itself."[15]

We can learn a final lesson from science that aids us in understanding faith: the evolution of a nasty little creature that can be found in questionable foods such as poorly processed pork and "gas-station sushi": the tapeworm. The tapeworm has evolved from a much more complex organism to the form it has now. In its evolution it adopted a "less is more" approach to parasitism, losing its nervous system and its digestive system, leaving nothing but the ability to latch on to its prey and reproduce. Similarly, humans in hell would be those who cling to the lower form of existence rather than opening themselves up to the adventure of a new kind of life; they lose their capacity for anything beyond themselves.

The prospect of eternal damnation comes not from Christ but, rather, from us. As Joseph Ratzinger recognized, "Christ inflicts [damnation] on no one. In himself he is sheer salvation. Anyone who is with him has entered the space of deliverance and salvation. Perdition is not imposed by him, but comes to be wherever a person distances himself from Christ. It comes about whenever someone remains enclosed within himself."[16] The Christian life is the highest risk, but it ultimately offers the highest kind of fitness—if we live for love in Jesus Christ, then we open ourselves to everlasting life.

CONCLUSION: ORDER, OPENNESS, AND HOPE IN THE AGE OF THE VIRUS

As I type this conclusion, it is early October of the year 2020, and the human family is doing its best to survive a bug even nastier than the tapeworm.[1] We are living in the Age of the Virus, unprecedented in scope and in impact on every facet of life, affecting everyone and every relationship. COVID-19 is, in a negative sense, truly catholic according to the root meaning of the word: it pertains to the whole person and every person, indeed to the entire human family. Unlike the Church, it carries not the universal promise of life but the threat of death. And yet here's a stunning paradox: although this virus threatens our lives, we live because of yet another virus, which threatened life 150 million years ago and became the very lifeline that has sustained the life of every human being.

Genomic research has discovered that human DNA and the genomes of all mammals contain leftover viral DNA that infected egg and sperm cells in the distant past. Eight percent of the human genome is retroviral and is sometimes referred to as the "junk drawer" of our genetic code. Retroviruses have an amazing and mostly lethal feature: they can insert genetic code into cells while blocking the host cell from returning the favor. Around 150 million years ago, one such infection left behind this very feature in the genome of one of our mammalian ancestors and became a part of our inherited functional DNA. Through the trial and error process of evolution, *the placenta*, the key to the protection and nourishment of embryos in the womb, was "born" from the remnants of this virus, which triggered a genetic mutation that changed the DNA passed along to future generations.[2] Viruses bring disorder and death, and yet in this case, viral DNA became a key source of order and a new way of producing life, a way through which every human being is nourished and brought into the world.

This is by no means a singular, lonely example of evolutionary good fortune; it is a hallmark of our universe as understood through modern science. Emergent systems, arising from things much simpler and displaying new levels of complexity, distinguish our universe as one that is not closed and clocklike but open and often unpredictable. Science has revealed the universe to be a balance of order and openness, law and flexibility, symmetry and surprises. A fundamental order exists, but this order is flexible in ways that are open to the emergence of new, truly surprising levels of order. In this case, the biological tie between mother and child is the new level of order that came from an otherwise destructive viral invader.

Let's not pass this by too quickly, for there is no more theologically evocative biological reality, no greater symbol of divine grace, than the placenta. In a 2019 article of the online journal of the McGrath Institute for Church Life, scientist Kristin Collier captured this in a way that weds science and faith:

> In a mother's womb following conception, God is
> building between mother and child an anatomic mas-
> terpiece, a *relational organ*, that can only be described as
> amazing: the human placenta. Like God's hand reaching
> out for man as depicted in Michelangelo's art on the
> ceiling of the Sistine chapel, baby and mother can be
> thought of as reaching out for one another at a physio-
> logical level to build the placenta. The placenta is . . . a
> fetomaternal organ because it is made by both the baby
> and mother (and Providence).[3]

"And Providence"—what seems to be only chance, only trial and error to the unbelieving eye, is the mysterious, loving guidance of God, who brings about his plan in and through the causality of his creatures.

Here, in the evolution of the entire biosphere, and above all in the twisting trail of the evolution of human beings, we see the hallmark of the Holy Spirit, who, with the Father and the Son, creates the world. A few verses after Psalm 104 celebrates the universe being made in wisdom, the same psalm makes a prayerful plea: "Send forth your spirit . . . renew the face of the earth" (Ps 104:30). As we see vividly on the great day of Pentecost, the Holy Spirit is the source of openness and newness. Here we can see that faith has its own vision of openness that mutually resonates, like the tingling of wind chimes, with the universe's openness revealed by modern science.

According to St. John Paul II, "Through the Holy Spirit God exists in the mode of gift."[4] The greatest gifts are unmerited and involve the unexpected and unpredictable. The Spirit is also asso-ciated with love; as the apostle Paul writes, "The love of God has been poured out into our hearts through the holy Spirit that has been given to us" (Rom 5:5). Love, which is something freely given, is surprising when it is directed toward us by another, and it has the capacity to change our lives in new and unpredictable ways.

> The Holy Spirit, the divine person who is Gift-Love, is always associated with the new and surprising in God's work in history, when old patterns are taken up and brought to new levels not reducible to what went before. At the beginning of the universe, the Spirit is depicted as moving "over the waters" as new things are to be brought forth (Gen. 1:1). The Incarnation of the divine Son is a new event, expected by no one, not even by his own mother, who receives the Holy Spirit in order to conceive him in her womb: "The Holy Spirit will come upon you, and the power of the Most High will overshadow you: therefore the child to be born will be called holy, the Son of God" (Luke 1:34). And so, through Mary's "yes" to God and the overshadowing of the Holy Spirit, what it means to be human, the true way that God intends, is revealed in the life, death and resurrection of her Son.[5]

Mary herself becomes the *Theotokos* (God-bearer), the Mother of God according to his human nature—through the placenta that she and and her fully divine, fully human son, the Final Adam and our Savior, knitted together in the intimacy of her womb. And just as the Holy Spirit overshadowed Mary in the virginal conception of Christ, he was also at work far in advance when an ancient virus paved the way for the physiologic link between Mary and the incarnate Son of God, and between every mother and her unborn child.

It is the same Holy Spirit who also transforms this present moment and all moments, offering hope to believers precisely in the unanticipated and startling transformation of death into life, of sacrifice into strength, of sorrow into joy, and of disappointment into hope. As St. Paul writes, "Hope does not disappoint" (Rom 5:5). Can this example inspire hope in the Age of the Virus, both the coronavirus and the virus of societal fracture and division that stalk our world? It certainly can, but only if the bearers of the Spirit, the community of believers, are ready to proclaim the Gospel to our scientifically literate culture in a way that offers the amazing discoveries of modern science a wider, deeper foundation—the perspective of the eyes of faith—without diminishing the truth that science has discovered. St. John Paul II trailblazed this new path in 1988 when he wrote these words to the director of the Vatican Observatory: As we have already noted, St. John Paul II blazed this trail in 1988 by declaring that: "[s]cience can purify religion from error and superstition; religion can purify science from idolatry and false absolutes. Each can draw the other into a wider world, a world in which both can flourish."[6] It is when thinking believers follow him on this path, humbly and confidently allowing themselves to be informed and enriched by modern science, that science yields a new way in which the ageless wisdom of the Gospel can be proclaimed compellingly to the world. Through the contemplation of believers, led by the Holy Spirit, the diabolical misconception of conflict between the Catholic faith and modern science and the ideology of scientism can be transformed, like the viruses they are, into something life-giving: the integration of faith and reason.

In the same letter, St. John Paul II asked this hopeful question: "Does an evolutionary perspective bring any light to bear upon theological anthropology, the meaning of the human person as the image of God?" As we see in the case of the placenta and have hopefully seen throughout our journey in this book, the answer is a resounding "yes!" This example and this book can serve as a test case for the kind of theological reflection necessary for this crucial mission of evangelization. Thinking about divine creation, human personhood, and salvation in ways that are deeply informed by the contemporary sciences, the Church can overcome the echo chamber of self-enclosed theological language in which she can only speak to herself but not to the world. This mode of faith seeking understanding can offer ways for scientifically informed people to think about the Catholic faith in terms they understand. Moving beyond the seemingly impenetrable borders of secularism, the Church can realize, in the words of St. John Paul II, with "greater intensity the activity of Christ within her [in her mission of evangelization]: 'For God was in Christ, reconciling the world to himself' (2 Cor. 5:19)."

ACKNOWLEDGMENTS

There are many people who should be thanked for their support of this project. Above all, I want to thank Fr. James Socias, editor-in-chief, and the staff of Midwest Theological Forum for allowing me to adopt significant sections of the second edition of my textbook *Faith, Science and Reason: Theology on the Cutting Edge (FSR)*, published in December 2019. As a much more expansive text, much of the research and writing for FSR represented the most recent and best developed explanation of themes such as the doctrine of creation, the problem of evil, misunderstandings of evolution by believers, the nature and creation of the human soul, human sin, and Christ as the new and Final Adam. Adapting some of my best writing from the textbook for a more general readership allowed me to add new explanations and additional ideas that make *Creation: A Catholic's Guide to God and the Universe* something unique.

I also am indebted to friends who read the text and offered helpful comments and challenged me to push beyond previous work, especially Heidi Radabaugh, MA and Fr. Nathan O'Halloran, S.J., PhD.

Finally, I want to thank my wife Christine, my daughter Margaret, son-in-law Jean Paul, and my sons John, Peter, and William for their patience and encouragement.

NOTES

INTRODUCTION

1. This presentation was given on February 14, 2014, at a symposium for diocesan bishops and diocesan superintendents of Catholic education entitled "Science and Human Dignity," cosponsored by the USCCB and the McGrath Institute for Church Life, University of Notre Dame, South Bend, IN. The video of the presentation is available at: https://youtu.be/OaS1SV7xwWQ.

2. Mark Gray, "Young People Are Leaving the Faith. Here's Why," *Our Sunday Visitor Newsweekly,* August 27, 2016, https://www.osvnews.com/2016/08/27/young-people-are-leaving-the-faith-heres-why/.

3. St. John Paul II, Address to the Pontifical Academy of the Sciences (Spanish), October 3, 1981, http://www.vatican.va/content/john-paul-ii/es/speeches/1981/october/documents/hf_jp-ii_spe_19811003_accademia-scienze.html.

4. Benedict XVI, Easter Vigil Homily, April 23, 2011, http://w2.vatican.va/content/benedict-xvi/en/homilies/2011/documents/hf_ben-xvi_hom_20110423_veglia-pasquale.html.

5. Pope Francis, Address to the Pontifical Academy of the Sciences, October 27, 2014, http://w2.vatican.va/content/francesco/en/speeches/2014/october/documents/papa-francesco_20141027_plenaria-accademia-scienze.html.

6. Joseph Ratzinger, *"In the Beginning . . .": A Catholic Understanding of the Story of Creation and the Fall*, trans. Boniface Ramsey (Grand Rapids, MI: Eerdmans, 1986), 79–80.

7. St. John Paul II, Message to the Reverend George V. Coyne, S.J., Director of the Vatican Observatory, June 1, 1988, http://inters.org/John-Paul-II-Coyne-Vatican-Observatory.

1. LOVE IS THE REASON

1. Meister Eckhart, *Meister Eckhart: A Modern Translation*, translated by Raymond Bernard Blakney (New York: HarperPerennial, 2004), 245.

2. Douglas Adams, *The Restaurant at the End of the Universe* (New York: Macmillan, 1980), 1.

3. *Catechism of the Catholic Church*, 2nd ed. (Washington, DC: United States Catholic Conference, 2000), nos. 888–92. (Hereafter abbreviated as "*CCC.*")

4. "[S]i comprehendis, enim non est deus." St. Augustine, *Sermo 52*, 16: PL 38, 360 [translation mine].

5. Nicholas of Cusa, *De Deo Abscondito*, 1, 6, in Jasper Hopkins, ed. and trans., *A Miscellany of Nicholas of Cusa* (Minneapolis, MN: Arthur J. Banning Press, 1994), 300–311.

6. Jonathan Sacks, *The Great Partnership: Science, Religion, and the Search for Meaning* (New York: Schocken Books, 2011), 2.

7. St. John Paul II, Address to Participants in a Colloquium on Science, Philosophy, and Theology, September 5, 1986. http://www.vatican.va/content/john-paul-ii/fr/speeches/1986/september/documents/hf_jp-ii_spe_19860905_colloquio-scienza.html.

8. G. K. Chesterton, *Orthodoxy*, Moody Classics, new ed. (Chicago: Moody, 2009), 92.

9. St. Thomas Aquinas, *Summa Theologiae* III.101.1 (Hereafter referred to as "Aquinas, *ST.*")

10. Richard C. Lewontin, "Billions and Billions of Demons," *New York Times Book Review*, January 9, 1997, http://www.nybooks.com/articles/1997/01/09/billions-and-billions-of-demons/.

11. Christopher Hitchens, *God Is Not Great: How Religion Poisons Everything* (New York: Hachette Book Group, 2009), 282.

12. St. John Paul II, General Audience, January 15, 1986, http://inters.org/John-Paul-II-Catechesis-Heaven-Earth.

13. "Non coerceri maximo, contineri tamen a minimo, divinum est." As quoted in Joseph Ratzinger, *Introduction to Christianity*, trans. J. R. Foster and Michael J. Miller (San Francisco: Ignatius Press, 2004), 146.

14. Stephen Hawking, *Brief Answers to the Big Questions* (New York: Bantam Books, 2018), 38.

15. Stephen Barr, *The Believing Scientist: Essays on Science and Religion* (Grand Rapids, MI: William B. Eerdmans Publishing Company, 2016), 124.

16. William Shakespeare, *Romeo and Juliet*, Act I, Prologue.

17. Benedict XVI, Inaugural Homily, April 24, 2005, w2.vatican.va/content/benedict-xvi/en/homilies/2005/documents/hf_benxvi_hom_20050424_inizio-pontificato.html.

18. Benedict XVI, Meeting with the Clergy of the Dioceses of Belluno-Feltre and Treviso in Auronzo di Cadore, July 24, 2007, w2.vatican.va/content/benedict-xvi/en/speeches/2007/july/documents/hf_ben-xvi_spe_20070724_clero-cadore.html.

19. Vatican I, Dogmatic Constitution on the Catholic Faith *Dei Filius*, April 24, 1870, chap. 1, nos. 2–3, https://www.ewtn.com/library/councils/v1.htm#4.

20. *CCC*, no. 310.

21. International Theological Commission, "Communion and Stewardship: Human Persons Created in the Image of God," July 23, 2004, no. 66, http://www.vatican.va/roman _curia/congregations/cfaith/cti_documents/rc_con_cfaith _doc_20040723_communion-stewardship_en.html. (Hereafter referred to as ITC, "Communion and Stewardship".)

22. Ecumenical Council of Florence, *Bull of Union with the Copts*, 1442, http://www.ewtn.com/library/COUNCILS /FLORENCE.HTM.

23. St. Thomas Aquinas, *On Ephesians* 2.2.

24. Julian of Norwich, *Revelations of Divine Love*, chap. 5.

25. For a complete translation of the *Enûma Eliš* online, go to www.sacred-texts.com/ane/enuma.htm.

26. Joseph Ratzinger, *"In the Beginning . . .": A Catholic Understanding of the Story of Creation and the Fall*, trans. Boniface Ramsey (Grand Rapids, MI: Eerdmans, 1986),3.

2. THE POPE AND THE QUESTION

1. Benedict XVI, Inaugural Homily, April 24, 2005, w2.vatican.va/content/benedict-xvi/en/homilies/2005 /documents/hf_benxvi_hom_20050424_inizio-pontificato.html.

2. Benedict XVI, "Address, Visit to the Auschwitz Camp," Auschwitz-Birkenau, May 28, 2006, http://www.vatican.va /content/benedict-xvi/en/speeches/2006/may/documents/hf _ben-xvi_spe_20060528_auschwitz-birkenau.html.

3. Herbert McCabe, *God Matters* (London: Geoffrey Chapman, 1987), 26.

4. St. Augustine, *Confessions* 7.3, 5.

5. St. Augustine, *City of God* 11.22.

6. Ecumenical Council of Florence, *Bull of Union with the Copts*, 1442.

7. W. Norris Clarke, S.J., *The One and the Many: A Contemporary Thomistic Metaphysics* (Notre Dame, IN: University of Notre Dame Press, 2001), 7.

8. Adapted from Clarke, *The One and the Many*, 283.

9. Paul VI, General Audience, November 15, 1972, https://www.ewtn.com/catholicism/library/confronting-the-devils-power-8986.

10. François Mauriac, foreword to Elie Wiesel, *Night* (New York: Farrar, Straus and Giroux, 2006), xvii–xxi.

3. A FREELY EVOLVING UNIVERSE

1. C. S. Lewis, *The Silver Chair,* book 4 in The Chronicles of Narnia series (New York: Scholastic, 1987), 21.

2. St. Augustine, *City of God* 19.4.

3. Dennis Bonnette, *Origin of the Human Species*, 2nd ed. (Ypsilanti, MI: Sapientia Press, 2003), 55.

4. Conor Cunningham, *Darwin's Pious Idea: Why the Ultra-Darwinists and Creationists Both Get It Wrong* (Grand Rapids, MI: Eerdmans, 2010), 144.

5. Cunningham, *Darwin's Pious Idea*, 147.

6. "Convergence: Marsupials and Placentals," PBS LearningMedia, accessed April 12, 2021, https://illinois.pbslearningmedia.org/resource/tdc02.sci.life.evo.convergence/convergence-marsupials-and-placentals/.

7. Ian Curran, "Headed toward Christ: The Grand Narrative of Evolution," review of Simon Conway Morris, *The Runes of Evolution: How the Universe Became Self-Aware* (West Conshohocken, PA: Templeton Press, 2015), in *The Christian Century*, March 17, 2016.

8. Simon Conway Morris, *Life's Solution: Inevitable Humans in a Lonely Universe* (Cambridge: Cambridge University Press, 2003), 310.

9. Morris, *Life's Solution*, 20.

10. Erich Wasmann, "Evolution," in *The Catholic Encyclopedia*, vol. 5 (New York: The Gilmary Society, 1909), 654. Francisco Suárez (1548–1617) was a Jesuit theologian and philosopher.

11. St. Augustine, *De Trinitate* 3.9.16. (*The Trinity*, trans. Edmund Hill, WSA I/5 [Hyde Park, NY: New City, 1991]).

12. St. Augustine, *De Genesi* 6.16.22. (*On Genesis*, trans. Edmund Hill, WSA I/13 [Hyde Park, NY: New City], 2002). (Hereafter referred to as St. Augustine, *De Genesi*.)

13. St. Augustine, *De Genesi* 6.13.23.

14. St. Augustine, *De Genesi* 6.16.23.

15. John Henry Newman, *Philosophical Notebooks*, vol. 2, December 9, 1863.

16. Aquinas, *ST* I.67.4 *ad* 3.

17. Ernan Mcmullin, "Darwin and the Other Christian Tradition," *Zygon* (46: 2011): 311-312.

18. *CCC*, no. 1062.

4. A COUPLE IN A CAVE?

1. See Francisco J. Ayala, "The Myth of Eve: Molecular Biology and Human Origins," *Science* 270 (1995): 1930–36.

2. ACTS Apologist, "Adam, Eve, and Anthropology," *ACTS Apologist Blog*, June 8, 2019, emphasis mine, http://actsapologist.blogspot.com/2019/06/adam-eve-and-anthropology.html.

3. Dennis R. Venema and Scot McKnight, *Adam and the Genome: Reading Scripture after Genetic Science* (Grand Rapids, MI: Brazos Press, 2017), 62–65.

4. ACTS Apologist, "Adam, Eve, and Anthropology."

5. Pius XII, *Humani generis*, August 12, 1950, no. 37, http://www.vatican.va/content/pius-xii/en/encyclicals/documents/hf_p-xii_enc_12081950_humani-generis.html.

6. Vatican II, Dogmatic Constitution on the Church *Lumen Gentium*, November 21, 1964, chap. 3, no. 25, https://www.vatican.va/archive/hist_councils/ii_vatican_council/documents/vat-ii_const_19641121_lumen-gentium_en.html

7. Francis A. Sullivan, S.J., *Magisterium: Teaching Authority in the Catholic Church* (Dublin: Gill and Macmillan, 1983), 166. For a more complete consideration, see Avery Cardinal Dulles, *Magisterium: Teacher and Guardian of the Faith* (Naples, FL: Sapientia, 2007), 83–99.

8. "The archival records make clear that the non-definitive language was deliberately chosen over the stronger language of early drafts of the encyclical." Kenneth W. Kemp, "Adam and Eve and Evolution," Society of Catholic Scientists, accessed April 13, 2021, https://www.catholicscientists.org/idea/adam-eve-evolution.

9. Joseph Ratzinger, *Schöpfungslehre* (1964), 253, cited in Santiago Sanz, "Joseph Ratzinger y la doctrina de la creación. Los apuntes de Münster de 1964 (y III): Algunos temas debatidos," *Revista Española de Teología* 74 (2014): 453–96 at 493n126, emphasis mine, (English translation is from a forthcoming monograph on Ratzinger and evolution by Matthew J. Ramage). For a summary and discussion of Professor Ratzinger's unpublished lecture notes (*Vorlesungsmitschriften*) housed at the Institut Papst Benedikt XVI in Regensburg, see Santiago Sanz, "The Manuscripts of Joseph Ratzinger's Lectures on the Doctrine of Creation," trans. Matthew J. Ramage, *Nova et Vetera*, forthcoming.

10. Benedict XVI, Easter Vigil Homily, April 23, 2011, http://w2.vatican.va/content/benedict-xvi/en/homilies/2011/documents/hf_ben-xvi_hom_20110423_veglia-pasquale.html.

11. Joseph Ratzinger, *"In the Beginning . . .": A Catholic Understanding of the Story of Creation and the Fall*, trans. Boniface Ramsey (Grand Rapids, MI: Eerdmans, 1986), 43–44.

12. St. John Paul II, General Audience, April 16, 1986.

13. ITC, "Communion and Stewardship," no. 70.

14. Joseph Ratzinger, *Dogma and Preaching: Applying Christian Doctrine to Daily Life*, 2nd ed. (San Francisco: Ignatius Press, 2017), 141–42.

15. St. John Paul II, General Audience, January 2, 1980, https://www.ewtn.com/library/papaldoc/jp2tb13.htm.

16. ITC, "Communion and Stewardship," no. 66.

17. Joseph Ratzinger, *The God of Jesus Christ: Meditations on the Triune God*, 2nd ed., trans. Brian McNeil (San Francisco: Ignatius Press, 2006), 59–60.

5. FROM BLOMBOS CAVE TO BETHLEHEM

1. Christopher S. Henshilwood et al., "Emergence of Modern Human Behavior: Middle Stone Age Engravings from South Africa," *Science* 295 (February 15, 2002): 1278–80. Since this first discovery, Henshilwood has found several similar artifacts, including a cross-hatch drawing made with an ochre crayon on a piece of silcrete; cf. Christopher S. Henshilwood et al., "An Abstract Drawing from the 73,000-Year-Old Levels at Blombos Cave, South Africa," *Nature* 562 (September 12, 2018): 115–18.

2. Ian Tattersall, *Masters of the Planet: The Search for Our Human Origins* (New York: Palgrave-Macmillan, 2012), 63–64, 199.

3. Tattersall, *Masters,* 203.

4. Conor Cunningham, *Darwin's Pious Idea: Why the Ultra-Darwinists and Creationists Both Get It Wrong* (Grand Rapids, MI: Eerdmans, 2010), 187.

5. *CCC*, "Glossary"; cf. *CCC*, no. 1935.

6. Mark Schwartz, "People from Distant Lands Have Strikingly Similar Genetic Traits, Study Reveals," *Stanford Report*, January 8, 2003, https://news.stanford.edu/news/2003/january8/genetics-18.html.

7. Tattersall, *Masters,* 194.

8. Lisa K. Fazio et al., "Knowledge Does Not Protect against Illusory Truth," *Journal of Experimental Psychology* 144, no. 5 (2015): 993–1002.

9. Emanuel Maidenberg, "Why We Believe What We're Told," *Psychology Today*, June 27, 2017, https://www.psychologytoday.com/us/blog/belief-and-the-brain/201706/why-we-believe-what-we-re-told.

10. Elizabeth Culotta, "Roots of Racism," *Science*, May 18, 2012, http://science.sciencemag.org/content/336/6083/825.full.

11. Kenneth R. Miller, *The Human Instinct: How We Evolved to Have Reason, Consciousness, and Free Will* (New York: Simon & Schuster, 2018), 130–31.

12. Aquinas, *ST* I–II.85.6.

13. Alasdair MacIntyre, *Dependent Rational Animals: Why Human Beings Need the Virtues*, Paul Carus Lecture Series 20 (Chicago: Open Court, 1999), 53–55. Cf. Aquinas, *De Veritate* 24.2; *ST* I.84.1.

14. Aquinas, *ST* I.97.1.

15. Aquinas, *ST* I.95.2.

16. Ian Tattersall, *The Strange Case of the Rickety Cossack: and Other Cautionary Tales from Human Evolution* (New York: St. Martin's Press, 2015), 219.

17. Nicholas Lombardo, "Original Sin, Evolution and Death" (paper presented at the Academy of Catholic Theology Annual Conference, Washington Retreat Center, Washington, DC, May 20, 2014).

18. Joseph Ratzinger, *Schöpfungslehre* (1964), cited in Santiago Sanz, "Joseph Ratzinger y la doctrina de la creación. Los apuntes de Münster de 1964 (y III): Algunos temas debatidos," *Revista Española de Teología* 74 (2014): 453–96 at 493n126, (English translation is from a forthcoming monograph on Ratzinger and evolution by Matthew J. Ramage.)

19. St. Irenaeus, *Against Heresies*, V.6.1.

20. Aquinas, *ST* I–II.91.6 resp.

21. Tattersall, *The Strange Case*, 219.

22. Henri Rondet, *Original Sin: The Patristic and Theological Background* (New York: Alba House, 1972), 166–67, emphasis mine.

23. *CCC*, nos. 397–98, emphasis mine.

24. *CCC*, no. 400.

25. *CCC*, no. 401.

26. *CCC*, nos. 404–5.

27. St. Paul VI, *Solemni hac Liturgia* (*Credo of the People of God*), no. 16, June 30, 1968, http://w2.vatican.va/content /paul-vi/en/motu_proprio/documents/hf_p-vi_motu-proprio _19680630_credo.html.

28. Aquinas, *ST* I–II.81.1, resp.

29. Joseph Ratzinger, *"In the Beginning . . .": A Catholic Understanding of the Story of Creation and the Fall*, trans. Boniface Ramsey (Grand Rapids, MI: Eerdmans, 1986), 73.

30. Benedict XVI, Homily on the Feast of the Immaculate Conception, December 8, 2005, http://w2.vatican.va/content/benedict-xvi/en/homilies/2005/documents/hf_ben-xvi_hom_20051208_anniv-vat-council.html.

31. Benedict XVI, Homily on the Feast of the Immaculate Conception.

32. Vatican II, Dogmatic Constitution on Divine Revelation *Dei Verbum*, November 8, 1965, chap. 2, no. 8, https://www.vatican.va/archive/hist_councils/ii_vatican_council/documents/vat-ii_const_19651118_dei-verbum_en.html.

33. Ratzinger, *Schöpfungslehre* (1964), 252; Sanz, "Joseph Ratzinger y la doctrina de la creación. Los apuntes de Münster de 1964 (y III)," 484n90. (Trans., Matthew Ramage.)

34. Second Vatican Council, *Gaudium et Spes*, December 7, 1965, no. 22, emphasis mine, https://www.vatican.va/archive/hist_councils/ii_vatican_council/documents/vat-ii_const_19651207_gaudium-et-spes_en.html.

35. *CCC*, no. 365.

36. Joseph F. X. Sladky, "St. Peter Claver: Slave of the Slaves Forever," *Crisis Magazine*, September 8, 2014, https://www.crisismagazine.com/2014/st-peter-claver-slave-slaves-forever.

37. Rodney Stark, *The Rise of Christianity: How the Obscure, Marginal Jesus Movement Became the Dominant Religious Force in the Western World in a Few Centuries* (New York: HarperOne, 1996), 215.

6. FROM EVOLUTION TO RESURRECTION

1. ITC, "Communion and Stewardship," no. 53.

2. John Behr, *Becoming Human: Meditations on Christian Anthropology in Word and Image* (Crestwood, NY: St. Vladimir's Seminary Press, 2013), 34.

3. St. Irenaeus, *Against Heresies* IV.34.1, as quoted in Roch Kereszty, *Jesus Christ: Fundamentals of Christology*, 3rd ed. (Staten Island, NY: Society of St. Paul's, 2018), 200.

4. Behr, *Becoming Human*, 35.

5. St. Ignatius of Antioch, *Letter to the Romans* IV.

6. St. Augustine, *De civitate Dei* 10.6, as quoted in Kereszty, *Jesus Christ*, 212.

7. Cf. *Lumen gentium*, nos. 14–16.

8. Pope Benedict XVI, *Deus Caritas Est*, December 25, 2005, no. 1, http://w2.vatican.va/content/benedict-xvi/en/encyclicals/documents/hf_ben-xvi_enc_20051225_deus-caritas-est.html.

9. Benedict XVI, *Jesus of Nazareth: Holy Week: From the Entrance into Jerusalem to the Resurrection* (San Francisco: Ignatius Press, 2011), 244.

10. Joseph Ratzinger, *Eschatology: Death and Eternal Life*, 2nd ed. (Washington, DC: Catholic University of America Press, 1988), 238.

11. Conor Cunningham, "Why Study Life before Death with Conor Cunningham," YouTube, September 26, 2016, https://www.youtube.com/watch?v=McZMBqw8bb8.

12. Flannery O'Connor, *The Habit of Being: Letters of Flannery O'Connor*, selected and edited by Sally Fitzgerald (New York: Farrar, Straus & Giroux, 1979), 100.

13. Paul Haffner, *Mystery of Creation* (Herefordshire, UK: Gracewing, 1995), 104.

14. Benedict XVI, *Jesus of Nazareth: Holy Week*, 246–47.

15. Robert Barron, *The Strangest Way: Walking the Christian Path* (Maryknoll, NY: Orbis Books, 2002), 75.

16. Joseph Ratzinger, *Eschatology: Death and Eternal Life,* 2nd ed. (Washington, DC: Catholic University of America Press, 1988), 205.

CONCLUSION

1. A version of this epilogue also appeared under the title "The Holy Spirit, Modern Science and the Mission of Evangelization" in *Evangelization and Culture: The Journal of the Word on Fire Institute* (6: Winter 2020): 51–54.

2. Jamie Henzy, "Retroviruses, the Placenta and the Genomic Junk Drawer," *Small Things Considered*, June 2, 2014, http://schaechter.asmblog.org/schaechter/2014/06/retroviruses-the-placenta-and-the-genomic-junk-drawer.html.

3. Kristin Collier, "Some Human Beings Carry Remnants of Other Humans in Their Bodies," *Church Life Journal*, July 25, 2019, https://churchlifejournal.nd.edu/articles/human-beings-carry-remnants-of-other-humans-in-their-bodies/.

4. St. John Paul II, *Dominum et Vivificantem*, May 18, 1986, no. 10, http://www.vatican.va/content/john-paul-ii/en/encyclicals/documents/hf_jp-ii_enc_18051986_dominum-et-vivificantem.html.

5. Christopher T. Baglow, *Faith, Science, and Reason: Theology on the Cutting Edge*, 2nd ed. (Downers Grove, IL: Midwest Theological Forum, 2019), 1–15.

6. St. John Paul II, Message to the Reverend George V. Coyne, S.J., Director of the Vatican Observatory, June 1, 1988, http://inters.org/John-Paul-II-Coyne-Vatican-Observatory.

Christopher T. Baglow is the director of the Science and Religion Initiative in the McGrath Institute for Church Life at the University of Notre Dame, where he also serves as a professor in the theology department. He is the author of the textbook *Faith, Science, & Reason*, and his work has been featured by the Word on Fire Institute and in *That Man is You*, *Crux*, and *Church Life Journal*. He is a consultant for the USCCB Committee on Catechesis and Evangelization, and his thirty-year career in Catholic education has spanned high school, undergraduate, graduate, and seminary teaching.

Baglow earned a bachelor's degree from Franciscan University of Steubenville, a master's degree from the University of Dallas, and a doctorate from Duquesne University. He is a member of the Society of Catholic Scientists and a theological liaison to the board. He is a member of the Academy of Catholic Theology and the Catholic Theological Society of America.

He was awarded grants from the John Templeton Foundation for his work helping Catholic educators integrate faith and science in their classrooms, most notably for creating and directing the Steno Learning Program in Faith and Science (named for Blessed Nicholas Steno) and the Integrating Faith and Science at Catholic High Schools Nationwide project.

Baglow and his wife, Christine, were honored with the Servus Fidelis Award for service to the Church in faith and marriage ministries and with the Ray Mock Memorial Award for lifetime achievement in youth ministry. Baglow was one of four people to receive an Expanded Reason Award for Teaching from the University of Francisco de Vitoria and the Vatican–Joseph Ratzinger Foundation.

He lives with his family in the South Bend, Indiana, area.

The McGrath Institute for Church Life was founded as the Center for Pastoral and Social Ministry by the late Notre Dame President Fr. Theodore Hesburgh, C.S.C., in 1976. The McGrath Institute partners with Catholic dioceses, parishes, and schools to provide theological education and formation to address pressing pastoral problems. The Institute connects the Catholic intellectual life to the life of the Church to form faithful Catholic leaders for service to the Church and the world. The McGrath Institute strives to be the preeminent source of creative Catholic content and programming for the new evangelization.

https://mcgrath.nd.edu/

MORE IN THE
ENGAGING CATHOLICISM SERIES

Books in the Engaging Catholicism series from the McGrath Institute for Church Life at the University Notre Dame help readers discover the beauty and truth of the Catholic faith through a concise exploration of the Church's most important but often difficult-to-grasp doctrines as well as crucial pastoral and spiritual practices. Perfect for seekers and new Catholics, clergy and catechetical leaders, and everyone in between, the series expands the McGrath Institute's mission to connect the Catholic intellectual life at Notre Dame to the pastoral life of the Church and the spiritual needs of her people.

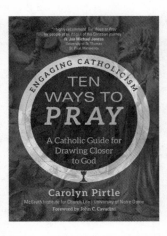

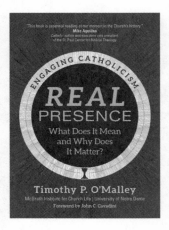